In Support of Education
The Functioning of Local Government

The Joseph Rowntree Foundation has supported this project as part of its programme of research and innovative development projects, which it hopes will be of value to policy makers and practitioners. The facts presented and views expressed in this report, however, are those of the researchers and not necessarily those of the Foundation.

In Support of Education
The Functioning of Local Government

Philippa Cordingley and Maurice Kogan

Jessica Kingsley Publishers
London and Philadelphia

First published in the United Kingdom in 1993 by
Jessica Kingsley Publishers Ltd
116 Pentonville Road
London N1 9JB

Copyright © 1993 Philippa Cordingley and Maurice Kogan

British Library Cataloguing in Publication Data
Cordingley, Philippa
In Support of Education: The Functioning of
Local Government
I. Title II. Kogan, Maurice
379.42
ISBN 1-85302-536-4

Printed and Bound in Great Britain by
Cromwell Press, Melksham, Wiltshire

Contents

List of Tables

List of Figures

Acknowledgements

This book is the result of a project funded by the Joseph Rowntree Foundation on the Functioning of Local Government. It concentrates on the particular case of education which has encountered the most radical changes of all of the public services as a result of successive government actions.

The fieldwork for the study was undertaken in the LEA areas of Coventry, Hertfordshire and Warwickshire and we wish to express our particular thanks to the Chief Education Officers and Chairs of those three LEAs, together with their colleagues and those in the schools, colleges and other institutions in the areas who participated in our study. We are also grateful to those who made time to attend our national consultation held in London in October 1992.

Throughout our study we were helped by first Peter John and then Pat Kneen of the Joseph Rowntree Foundation and were particularly fortunate in the expert advice and critical encouragement offered us by our Advisory Group.

Our most particular thanks go, however, to two colleagues at Brunel. Valerie Beale not only administered the project in all of its complex stages but was also a partner in our fieldwork and analytic development of the project. Without her expertise and commitment, the project would never have been completed in so short a time. We were also fortunate in the choice of a research assistant, Catherine Ardouin, who worked for us on a student placement from the Faculty of Social Sciences at Brunel for a period of nearly six months. She made a substantial contribution to both the data analysis and the administration of the project. We are indebted to our project secretaries, Marie Heard, Jo Wright and Caroline Large for their expert production of texts.

The members of our Advisory Group were:

Sir Charles Carter (Chairman) (Trustee, Joseph Rowntree Foundation)

Professor Eric Bolton (formerly Senior Chief Inspector, DES, now London University Institute of Education)

Ms Margaret Maden (County Education Officer, Warwickshire County Council)

Dr Robert Morris (formerly Education Secretary, Association of Metropolitan Authorities, now Open University)

Sir Peter Newsam (Director, London University Institute of Education)

Dr Norma Raynes (Campaign for the Advancement for State Education)

Professor Sue Richards (Office for Public Management)

Professor Alec Ross (University of Lancaster)

Pat Kneen (Senior Research Officer, Joseph Rowntree Foundation)

CHAPTER 1

The Argument

Government action is reducing and calling into question the role of local education authorities (LEAs). Its impacts are likely to be enormous. This book is an account of a project which attempts to analyse the needs which must be met if the education service is to perform its functions properly, and the extent to which LEAs are necessary.

In this book we therefore tackle the question: do schools and other providers of education require any entity beyond themselves, other than the central authorities, in order to perform their functions? In pursuing it we decided to follow a logical path which would make it possible to compare the ingredients and outcomes of different forms of governance.[1] In this and succeeding chapters we will identify the relevant components of models of governance in the following sequence:

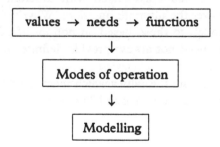

values → needs → functions
↓
Modes of operation
↓
Modelling

VALUES

We begin with asking what are the values that are endorsed in education. Later, in Chapter 5, we see how far different values might be endorsed by different models of governance.

Why are values important? Values derive their status from the fact that people are prepared to advocate or defend them, because they satisfy their

---

[1] Throughout the text we have used the word 'governance' because our models are concerned with the processes rather than the structures of governing.

moral propensities and sense of what feels right. Value propositions may be reinforced by warnings of the consequences of not following them – that, for example, a failure to ensure fair distribution (the equality value) will lead to discontent, malfunctioning or revolution. But many have advanced the value of equality without justification. Justifications from likely outcomes are second order or instrumental defences of basic value positions which emanate, in D.H. Lawrence's phrase, more from the solar plexus than the reason. Values are important because they are asserted and accepted and not because they provide logical or scientific explanations of actions. They affect actions rather than provide a prescriptive direction.

Choices in education are largely based upon concepts of what the good life and the good society should be; because education is so value imbued, the analysis of preferred values is an essential starting point for the interpretation of policies and the structures created to implement them. The analysis of values can inform the actions of policy makers (or their critics), their priorities and those affected by their policies. It may reveal inconsistencies in policies, or multiple value positions struggling for priority within a policy; many policies try to achieve more than one conflicting goal at once. It may also serve to separate rhetoric from substance in the sense that it helps identify that which is felt to be an irrefutable truth from that which is argued on evidence or fact.

In detecting the values associated with different policies, we are attempting to answer the ultimate question: 'Why?': Why, for example, prefer market models to those based on notions of public utility? The answers, however, need not always provide definite clues to the actions eventually taken.

In Chapter 5, we state the values which seem to underpin conceptual models of educational governance and illustrate their manifestation in the education system.

NEEDS AND WANTS

From identifying values, the next step in stripping down the components of the approaches to governance is an exploration of statements of needs and wants. In principle, all public institutions and systems deal with wants. These are either expressed by clients or interpreted by others; hitherto wants have usually been inferred by professionals and politicians or promoted by interest groups on clients' behalf. The untreated expression of wants rarely forms the stuff of educational provision and distribution. Wants are usually converted into statements of needs, which are, in effect authorised, or accepted, or legitimated, statements of wants. Some kind of governmental or administrative process takes place to ensure this conversion.

Identifying wants as needs and then assessing such needs involves value choices – what, for example, is to be preferred in attempting to establish a better educational destiny for people in an area? Increasingly, such value positions are being stated openly, whether they concern the advancement of the economy through the pursuit of excellence or the pursuit of equality through schemes of affirmative action. Even so, they are not often identified as explicit criteria for the justification of needs. Yet even where it is implicit and unclear, the effect of values on the determination of needs is no less present.

In Chapter 6 we will enumerate the needs presented by current educational policies and practices, and our fieldwork. We shall then identify the ways in which different governance arrangements emphasise or discount different needs and link the needs and their treatment to values, functions and interests.

FUNCTIONS

Functions are the most evident expression of values and needs to those who take part in, or are subject to, governance. The use of vocabulary is variable, but functions are the blocks of work which an educational institution or system will be committed to perform. They are broken down into tasks which are more specific as to limitations of time and work. Some functions will derive from legislative provision, either mandatory or permissive, and others from the policies of those who have power to decide what will be done. Others will form part of an unstated tradition of work; many functions are performed by professionals as discretionary tasks which emanate more from their training and professional culture than from explicit, authorised functions. As with needs, they emerge as a result of conflicting values and interests.

In Chapter 6, we link functions with needs. In doing so we offer a rationalistic and 'optimum' framework which places the lists of functions drawn from our fieldwork and from policy documents in a logical sequence.

The link between values and needs, and functions, whilst important, is likely to be unsystematic for there are inevitably gaps between intentions and achievements. And changes in values or perceptions of needs may take a long while to be translated into functions because so many of the elements of educational working are long-term – the schooling of an individual takes at least 11 years; teachers are in post a long time; assessment patterns take long to change; buildings are there almost forever, and so on. It is partly because of the difficulty in achieving a direct connection between values, needs and functions that functions appear to constitute both the purpose and the outcome of governance as well as its instrument.

MODALITIES

The separate elements of our analysis – values, needs and functions – are significant in their own right as well as important in terms of providing linkages between motivation, interpretation and action. But, in working reality, they are not rigorously interdependent. At the point of application, matters such as long and/or short term feasibility, interests, cost, style of relationship and power structures constrain or enhance particular values, needs or functions. The last elements in our analytic chain are therefore the operational modes, or modalities adopted in different forms of governance.

PUTTING CONCEPTS TO WORK: A RANGE OF MODELS OF GOVERNANCE

We propose the analysis of values, needs, functions and modes of operation as a framework for comparing approaches to governance. They also serve as criteria for evaluating them.

Like all those who examine or propose approaches to governance we have our own value stance. Our task in research and writing has been to find ways of working which reach beyond the limitations of single value systems. We believe that delineating a wide range of approaches against a rigorous, or at least explicit, conceptual framework enables both researcher and reader to face the most usual resistance to critique – 'they would say that wouldn't they' – and to explore rather than attack alternative possibilities.

In selecting relevant approaches for comparison we have constructed a series of models of governance which are being canvassed in the public services as a whole. We have also compared the post-1945 forms of education governance and the proposals in the White Paper, *Choice and Diversity* (1992) with those tackled in our analytic framework. The 1992 White Paper anticipates many of the provisions of the Education Bill,

1992 which was passing through Parliament, and therefore subject to further amendment, as this book was going to press.

The passing of the Education Reform Act 1988 (ERA) and its subsequent interpretation in central government guidance provide an alternative gloss on conceptual models and historical or currently proposed policy measures. Our fieldwork shows three LEAs interpreting the values, needs, functions and modalities implied by ERA in their own distinctive ways. Chapter 3 provides a summary of this application.

The array of models is offered not in the expectation that the present government will change its mind on recently legislated provisions, but in the knowledge that nothing is forever. Governing structures resulting from so decisive a revolution are likely to display faults and strains before long. New dispensations will evolve under the impress of realities experienced in the working life of schools and communities.

When the strains show, alternative thinking should be at hand. As present policies are implemented we hope that our modelling will provide a base for their critical evaluation. They might also reassure those in the field of educational administration, who have been subjected to what one seasoned observer has characterised as 'casual abuse', that it is not they who are out of step.

The models used fall into two groups.

COMMUNITY AGENCIES (CAs)

In these models public account for actions is made to a wide range of local stakeholders as well as to central government. Although public and local accountability suggests an elected base, this is a usual rather than a necessary precondition.

The professional-electoral model allows for power to be shared between governors, heads and teachers in the school and the professional and locally elected leadership of an intermediary body.

The multi-purpose public purchasing model allows for education policy to compete with other related, local, public services for resources and for education services to be coordinated with adjacent services. Its activities do not include providing services but are restricted to assessing local needs, specifying the quality, volume and cost of services and monitoring outcomes. Its multi-purpose nature implies an elected body, in order to legitimate the settlement of conflicting value preferences between service.

The single purpose public purchasing model would be the same as the multi-purpose purchasing model except that this would be an entity solely focused upon education. Local public accountability could, as in the health service, be carried out through direct reporting and consultation by an appointed or an elected intermediary board, or by a mixture of the two.

The individual school board model allows for power to be shared between central government and a largely autonomous individual school board concerned with a single institution. The requirement for local and public accountability, however, implies that the board would have an elected base although a mixture of elected and appointed members of a board could achieve the same end.

GOVERNMENT AGENCIES (GAs)

In some senses all public agencies are government agencies. The emphasis in these models is upon agencies which are publicly accountable to local communities only through central government.

The individual school board model would be the same as its community agency counterpart except that it would not make a formal, local public account. The board would therefore be appointed by central government and its autonomy would not be defended by a third party able to provide checks and balances.

In the funding council model the entity would be appointed through central government to whom it would report directly. In many other respects the model could be similar to the single purpose purchaser although there would be the possibility of acting as both provider and purchaser.

The individualistic model emphasises the individual client as purchaser. It would not concern itself in any detail with regulating providers or intermediary purchasers. Instead the emphasis would be on central government action to create and maintain as free a market as possible. Thus the decision about who should provide what would be made on the basis of aggregated individual choices exercised in choosing schools. In order to maximise choice and to allow the market to influence closure, the legal compulsion to provide, and to attend school, would need to be removed or at least significantly alleviated.

OTHER MODELS

There is a range of other possible models which have been examined briefly, and these are described in Chapter 4. They include the napoleonic and the professional models. We have not, however, built our analysis around these models since, in our judgement, it is not possible to conceive of them appearing as realistic possibilities within the next decade.

These models together with comparisons between their different treatments of values, needs, functions and modalities form the core of the critique of the contesting approaches to education governance. In this way we can ask, for example: 'What values do the LEAs in the traditional post-1945 model of operation espouse? How far would entities espousing provider/purchaser mechanisms be likely to match the perceived needs which they intended to meet? How far would individual school boards be able to match their functions to needs and values? Do some models meet perceived needs more effectively? At what cost in terms of values and functions?' And we can ask the same questions of the 1992 White Paper proposals.

CHAPTER 2

Contexts

THE CENTRAL GOVERNMENT CONTEXT

At any given time the State determines a settlement concerning what agencies will lie between itself and the individual. The acceptability of such arrangements is challenged from time to time and as a result the settlement is re-formulated. In the case of education, two agencies have been principally recognised by the state as intervening between the individual citizen's education and itself: the school and the local education authority (LEA).

The purpose of this chapter is to set our analysis of different approaches to the government of education in the context of the historic justifications and criticisms of local government.

HISTORY

For most of the last century there was consensus that 'A duty to provide services without the sensitivity caused by the presence of local democracy is local administration, not local government' (Redcliffe-Maud and Wood, 1974 p.22). Starting with the legislation of 1835 and 1888, local government has held a largely undisputed place in the working of the public services as testified by such widely different witnesses as J.S. Mill, Lord Salisbury, the Webbs, Joseph Chamberlain, Harold Laski, Lord Hailsham and Ken Livingstone.

Support for local government has derived from both positive and negative considerations:

- dislike of the clutter of private and privileged groups that hitherto had performed essential functions including adjudication of citizen's rights

- fear of an over-centralised state apparatus

- a belief that local groups should be able to re-interpret national interests

- proximity of control to those affected by services
- effectiveness of delivery
- the encouragement of democratic ways of working and thinking
- an emphasis on the needs of local society.

It was argued that local government was necessary to provide alternative modes of thinking and action to those provided by central government. As Mill (1912, p.368) put it :

'The very object of having local representation is in order that those who have an interest in common which they do not share with the general body of their countrymen may manage that joint interest by themselves'.

It has also been contended that local government would enhance the nature of the total democracy because central government tends, by nature, to be bureaucratic. Only a combination of, and contention between, local and central institutions with the central institutions of Parliament, Ministers and Departments, can ensure genuine democracy. There is plenty of evidence that local councils have used their independence to reflect local difference; indeed, this appears to be the source of some current government criticism of local government. Local government, even local government of the same political complexion as central government, is, to this cast of mind, creating unnecessary conflict by resisting or opposing national policy. To others it is precisely this manifestation of pluralism, the function of 'providing jagged edges to snag the smoothness of governmental power' (Hampton, 1987, p.4), which is a prime justification for local government. Local government has been thought to provide a focus for public activity, including listening, evaluating and social reporting. Local government is more sensitive to local conditions than is central government and is an alternative basis for responding to demand for public services that have no market.

In recent decades, however, there has been growing criticism of local government's working as a democratic form, of its politicisation, of its cost and of its effectiveness. Criticisms were formerly converted into attempts at improvement and reform; most recent legislation as it affects LEAs appears to be directed towards their substantial replacement.

The latest central initiatives on education and local government thus present a decisive break in the post-1945 settlement between central government and local education authorities – institutions which have been a part of British public life for over a century.

PURPOSES OF LOCAL GOVERNMENT

What is the nature of that which may be replaced? A collation of the many statements (e.g. Redcliffe-Maud, 1966-69; Sharpe, 1970) discussing or defining the purposes of local government will produce the following:

- to perform a wide range of tasks concerning the safety, health and well being of people in different localities
- to secure efficiency in the provision of services
- to fulfil the need to sustain a viable system of local democracy
- to attract and hold the interest of citizens in local matters
- to maintain a valid partnership with national authorities
- to adapt the services offered to changes in the lives of the community
- to provide a means whereby people can provide services for themselves.

The interpretation of these purposes has changed over time. For example, the concept of efficiency was based on a belief that services organised collectively and allowing for interconnection represented efficiency and that central government was too remote for it to be able to be well-informed enough to govern most services efficiently. But recently those arguments based on connectiveness have given away to those in which efficiency has meant minimisation of cost or value for money.

CHARACTERISTICS OF LOCAL GOVERNMENT

Local government's power and authority have rested on two principal features. First, it is legitimated and its autonomy justified because it is ruled by elected members. Those, however, who identify the shortcomings of local democratic governance or who disagree with the policies of particular councils contend that local elections confer a smaller degree of legitimacy than do general elections, if only because of the significantly smaller proportion of voters exercising their rights. Second, local government has the ability conferred by law to raise revenue. That second source of authority is weak in Britain because central government makes and implements legislation affecting local government.

A third set of issues has concerned the range of functions appropriate to local government. In the 1970s, the relatively simple concept of local government as an elected body capable of performing many of its functions in an integrated but self-contained fashion gave way to more complex conceptualisations. It was then accepted that its concerns related to networks outside itself and to changes in the economic and social structure involving both public agencies and private industry.

Some local authorities attempted, therefore, to widen their mandate to include economic development. But at the same time central government removed their control over such aspects of economic and social development as large scale urban planning, (as in Docklands). The training aspects of education and funding of what had been local authority sectors of higher and further education passed to centrally appointed funding agencies. These were perhaps the product of political preference rather than of a functional analysis. More fundamental thought has concerned the range of services provided by unitary or part unitary authorities. Over time boundaries have shifted as different doctrines on viability of service and proximity to clients have prevailed. This has in turn affected the size thought appropriate for local government units; it has been assumed, particularly since the late 1960s, that units must be large enough to provide services in an economic and competent manner.

The purposes of local government are multiple and its structure should reflect this. There is evidence, however, that connections between multiple services have been poorly made and an assertion that some professional services could be governed more effectively by separate entities; wherever possible by entities located as closely as possible to delivery.

Whilst there has been widespread agreement that a prime function of local government is to meet local needs, work to investigate such needs systematically and holistically and to interpret them openly has also been weak.

EVOLVING CRITICISMS OF LOCAL DEMOCRACY

Despite long established consensus that local democratic public services are necessary, from the late 1950s onwards the structure and working of English local government have been under virtually continuous review. A common thread of the earlier critique was the alleged inadequacy of the system to cope with the growing demands made on it as governments continued to extend the range of public services and as conditions of life were transformed (Redcliffe-Maud and Wood,1974).

Concern about the quality of the democratic process has also formed a continuing theme. Research undertaken for the Redcliffe-Maud Commission led them to conclude that many of the practical results continued to be 'disappointing' as a means of securing democratic representation (Redcliffe-Maud and Wood, 1974). Later on, criticism was centred on the somewhat formal and unresponsive nature of the democratic processes that it produced. Concepts of democracy moved from those of simple 'ballot-box' democracy, limited to the right to elect or refuse to elect councillors, to more diffuse and active concepts of accountability and control, responsiveness and the redress of grievance. Participation in decision-making was seen as involving far more elaborate modes of consultation than those implied by the right to vote for councillors every few years.

But democratic practice never seemed to catch up with democratic theory and so far from being regarded as the cure for a democratic deficit, local government was increasingly regarded by some as part of the disease. Modes of redress were created through such alternative mechanisms as the Local Government Commissioner and the enormously expanded use of judicial review.

Criticisms focused not only on the operation of the democratic basis of local government power and authority. Strong criticisms of local government's handling of local taxes were accompanied by increasing intervention in both the level and mode of collection of local taxes. Collection of local taxes for a range of local provision implies prioritisa-tion between services. In face of increasing financial constraint on local spending, some hard pressed service providers began to propose that education, the majority consumer of local council resources, should be freed from competition with other personal and social services. Some proposed that education was so important that it should be governed by a single purpose elected authority; for others the removal of competition between education and other local services would remove the justification for local tax raising and for their replacement by centrally determined funds.

But the argument that carried most weight with some central politi-cians was that LEAs, and their accomplices in the education estab-lishment, had failed to deliver education of an appropriate quality. The criticisms were thus lodged not only at local politicians but also at the LEA professionals.

It is thus clear that for all but the last ten years of the last century and a half, the case for local government has been taken for granted, but there has been constant concern about its efficacy. Recent policies have dis-carded the welfare state approach of deficiency funding, and the profes-sional analysis of needs. Central government values of efficiency and individual choice have required local government to move towards market forces and to shed some of its functions. Some of the mechanisms promoted to achieve such a shift, such as separating provision from the purchase of service and the local management of schools have, at the same time, addressed issues of efficacy and have received widespread support following initial antipathy.

But if the infrastructure of public education remains in the existence of publicly funded schools, the justification for an entity between the school and central government, for the formulation and delivery of educational services, is now the issue being faced. The questioning and criticism of the efficacy of local government have now reached a point where the existence of local education authorities, more than any other emanation of local government, is put in doubt. The arguments for local government noted in this chapter are thus put up to test and will find echoes in our analyses of values, needs and functions in succeeding chapters.

CHAPTER 3

The Project

AIMS

Our project is intended to identify the values, needs and functions implicit in different models of education governance. This was undertaken at a time when central government was drastically reducing LEA roles in education governance, management and administration.

METHODS

The project team worked in the areas of three local education authorities, of different sizes and nature, and interviewed a total of 92 participants occupying the positions as in Table 3.1.

Interviewees were selected both opportunistically (from those who might be available) and purposively to ensure reasonable coverage if the three authority areas were taken together.

The interviews were reinforced by reading relevant local authority and other documentation. The three field studies and the range of models were amplified and modified at three consultation meetings held in the three areas, and a national workshop where tabulations were also tested. These field based analyses were matched by examination of national legislation and policy pronouncements.

The interviews were semi-structured; that is, they were based on common schedules but the three interviewers were free to vary the emphasis according to the contribution made by the interviewee. The data were then collated on a computerized text analysis programme so that responses on each issue could be compared and conflated. The computerised text mounted to over 500 pages per authority which were reduced to reports and circulated to all of our interviewees who were invited to attend our three consultation meetings in the three areas. The schedules used in the interviews are reproduced in the Appendix.

Table 3.1 Participants in the project

Participants	Number of interviewees
County / Metropolitan Council Senior Officers	6
Education Committee Chairs	3
Education Department Senior Officers	18
LEA Inspectors / Advisors	3
Heads of Schools (maintained)	12
Heads of Schools (GM)	2
Principal of Colleges	3
Teachers / Lecturers	10
Education Social Workers	1
Pupils / Students	8
Careers Officers	3
TEC CE, board members	3
School Governors	15
Educational Psychologists	2
Other Organisations	2
DES Officers	1 informal unrecorded interview
HMI	none was permitted to be interviewed

We began our field work with schedules of questions about the needs of pupils, parents, communities and providers and about the organisational level at which they should be met. We also explored the justifications for the various alternative entities that might meet such needs. We were ultimately concerned with functions and types of governmental entities rather than with existing states.

Whilst the perceptions of our participants, who have to work in existing systems, could not provide a basis for exploring the full range of possible models, they do provide a base from which to consider the alternatives.

Our conceptual models and our three consultation exercises were the first stage in bridging the gap between what now exists, what our participants thought was required and the means of delivery.

The path from statements made by those engaged in education towards modelling and critique was thus:

1. Interviews with different groups within LEA areas, conflated to produce a range of opinions, on which needs of individuals, providers, and communities can be met by which entities, and on the relative priority of different needs.

2. Augmentation of individual views by discussion at three area seminars, by analysis of LEA and government policy papers, and by subsequent policy work in our three LEAs.

3. Conversion of (1) and (2) into tabulations of:

   • values
   • the entities which legitimise wants as needs
   • needs of individuals, communities and providers
   • functions of education entities.

4. Creation of models of educational governance. These have been derived from both the interviews and written materials and from identifying models that are present in current political discussion.

5. Testing of the models against the criteria set out in (3) and against modalities (i.e. economic, political, democratic, organisational, psychological and other criteria).

OUTCOMES OF THE PROJECT

The statement of needs, which was a principal target of our fieldwork, has been integrated into our analysis and is explained further in Chapter 6. The overall outcomes of our study derive from the needs, values, functions and modalities analysis and are stated in our conclusions. In addition, however, our fieldwork has illustrated, through a synthesis of our observations of education governance post-Education Reform Act (ERA), 1988, different approaches in three LEAs. We present this here before moving on to the more abstracted treatment of values, needs and functions.

Post-ERA approaches to governance: Coventry, Hertfordshire and Warwickshire

Both traditional and newly emerging approaches to education governance emphasise local diversity. It is unlikely, therefore, that there can be a typical LEA and our study was not intended to offer a representative sample. Nonetheless, the three LEAs presented here are distinctive: they offer a range of:

- size
- political orientation
- rural and urban needs
- styles of management
- types of school
- scales of budget
- expenditure priorities.

This range is illustrated by contrasting portraits of the characteristics of the three areas.

Quantitative distinctions between our three LEAs

The quantitative differences between the three LEAs are set out below:

The primary distinction between the three LEAs is the size of the population in the local authority area; Hertfordshire (975,000) having a population twice the size of Warwickshire (484,000) and over three times as large as Coventry (306,000), according to the 1991 Population Census.

In all of the three areas, approximately 7% of the population are under five years old, and 13% in the 5–15 age group. Coventry has a higher concentration of young adults; one quarter of its population is between the ages of 15 and 29, compared with one fifth in both Hertfordshire and Warwickshire. One fifth of each of the three areas' populations is between 30 and 44, 30% between 45 and 75, and 6% over 75 years of age.

Hertfordshire has significantly more schools than the other two local authorities; 545 compared to Warwickshire's 291 and Coventry's 143. Of these, Hertfordshire has eight grant-maintained schools and Warwickshire five. Coventry has no grant maintained schools at present.

With regard to Further Education (FE) colleges, there are five in Hertfordshire, four in Warwickshire, plus one college of agriculture, and four in Coventry.

School organisation varies significantly too. Hertfordshire provides nursery, primary, middle and secondary schools, whereas Coventry has nursery, primary and comprehensive secondary schools, as well as some separate infant and junior schools. Warwickshire's primary schools consist of first, infant, middle, junior, combined, and junior and infant schools, whilst its secondary schools comprise grammar, bilateral, comprehensive and high schools; also a separate Sixth form college. There are both single sex and co-educational schools in all three local authorities.

In selecting our three LEAs we sought variation in political control. The balance of the Councils and Education Committees is set out in Table 3.2 below which shows one Conservative Council and Education Committee, one Labour Council and Education Committee, and one Council

Table 3.2 Political balances of three LEAs

	Councils			Education Committees		
	Hertfordshire	Warwickshire	Coventry	Hertfordshire	Warwickshire	Coventry
Conservative	45	31	13	20	16	6
Labour	27	33	41	12	12	16
Lib. Democrat	5	4	0	2	2	0
Independent	0	3	0	0	1	0
TOTAL	77	71	54	34	31	22

with more Labour Councillors than Conservative Councillors, and more Conservative than Labour Education Committee members.

Although the percentage of surplus places based on standard numbers does not reflect genuinely surplus places and should be used with caution, it does provide a means of identifying the range of resources which might

Table 3.3 Percentage of surplus places

	Hertfordshire	Warwickshire	Coventry
Primary	21%	25%	17%
Secondary	16%	24%	23%

be caught up in maintaining plant and other maintenance costs across the LEAs. The percentages reported by each LEA are as follows:

Total Standard Spending Assessments (SSA) per head on education for the three authorities for 1992–93 were: Hertfordshire £379.35, Warwickshire £355.90, and Coventry £405.00.

Section 42 Statements were provided by the three local authorities for 1992–93. The General Schools Budget (GSB), which includes capital elements and is therefore subject to year in year fluctuation is, in Hertfordshire £289,375,000, in Warwickshire £139,609,776 and in Coventry £117,086,639. Of these, the Aggregated Schools Budget – the value of resources allocated to schools – as a percentage of the GSB in each area, is 72.6% in Hertfordshire, 71.8% in Warwickshire and 64.4% in Coventry.

A view of needs from three LEAs

From the quantitative dimensions, the path to qualitative comparison and illustrations of our three LEAs was initially through functions and modes of operation, since values inform educational governance and delivery implicitly rather than explicitly, and since functions and their effectiveness, rather than needs, are most immediately evident to those who have to work the system. And although our questions focused on needs, most respondents took as their starting point functions or modalities. Nonetheless they welcomed the opportunity to focus discussion upon needs; they recognised the importance of developing structures that would start from satisfying needs rather than the services as at present organised and were able either to identify and prioritise needs or to identify functions from which needs, and ultimately values, could be inferred. There was significant variation in the interpretation of the level of intensity of different needs. The following list (Table 3.4)encompasses all needs identified as 'irreducible' by a majority of respondents for *one or other* LEA, many of which were also identified as irreducible by a majority in *all three* LEAs.

This list is substantial but could be elaborated. It could also be challenged by some working outside education. It contains some surprising omissions such as innovation. It would be significantly shorter if those needs identified as irreducible by a majority across *all* LEAs were included. Some of the differences between LEAs can be explained by material differences in the characteristics of the area served; for example, support for small schools is promoted by LEAs with rural communities. Other issues excluded do not indicate so much different priorities as

Table 3.4 Needs identified as irreducible in our study

	Need identified as irreducible in:		Identified as irreducible and capable of delivery only by intermediary authority
	one or two LEAs	all three LEAs	

Needs tantamount to value statements

Ensuring compliance with statute	X		
Restraining undue selfishness	X		
Providing social justice		X	
Developing shared responsibilities		X	

Framework functions

Analysis of needs	X		
Data collection	X		
Support for small schools	X		
Organisational services	X		
Resource raising	X		
Capital programme specification	X		
Provision for vulnerable		X	
Strategic planning		X	
Quality assurance and performance indicators		X	
Providing a purchaser/ provider framework		X	
Resource allocation between purchasers/ providers		X	

Delivery functions

Educational services	X		
Statementing		X	
Appeals		X	
Specialist services		X	
INSET		X	
Exclusions		X	
Insurance		X	
Arbitration between HT and Governors		X	
Provision of sufficient places			X
Provision for those with special needs			X

differences of view about what schools can tackle. So, only in Hertfordshire, an LEA with a long track record of maximising devolution and open choice of school, is there a view that there is an irreducible need, beyond the school, to ensure compliance with statute; other areas assume schools could do this. Only in Warwickshire did a majority of our interviewees express the majority view that the schools and central government in partnership *could* (as opposed to should) carry out specifications for capital works.

But a more relevant test of the future role of LEAs or analogous bodies would be whether or not the majority of participants in all three areas could identify irreducible needs *that must be performed by an entity between the school and central government*. Only two needs met this test: provision of sufficient places and provision for those with special needs, although the need for an intermediary body to hear appeals or complaints against the school was also very strongly advocated elsewhere.

The difference between a majority view, a unanimous view and the nature of irreducibility was explored at each of the three local consultations on our findings. When pressed in this form, most governors, LEA officers, head teachers and parents were able and willing to distinguish between a strong desire that a need should be met by an intermediary body and a conviction that it must be met, and must be met at a particular level. There was often evidence of the disbenefits of neglecting particular needs. But it was recognised that an inclination towards particular needs and agencies reflected different value preferences and political choices.

Such dispositions also reflect the particular preoccupations current at the time of interviewing. A view of what constitutes effective governance is heavily affected by current issues, available competencies and established functions. For example, the fact that innovation was not mentioned reflects preoccupations with implementing externally imposed innovation and a view that, for some time, schools will need freedom from additional innovation in order to consolidate recent requirements. Furthermore, there is now a different mood in central government concerning innovation. Traditionally, government action and legislation have partly been judged on their durability and on their ability to produce stability to facilitate development over a significant period of time. The emphasis now is on the need to produce deep cultural change and, indeed, to espouse change as a goal in itself. Solutions are offered for test rather than for permanent installation. As a result, those running systems or institutions have no time to competently meet new requirements before they are required to take on another. Development is thus out.

Finally, we should note that our interviewees made a serious attempt to identify the needs which must be met, and some asserted that any system could be made to work. They also, however, pointed out that the cost of making some systems work is much greater in cash, quality or opportunity terms and that many of the most desirable options seemed excluded by the present debate.

Post-ERA Structures

The context at the time of interviewing was shaped predominantly by the provisions of ERA (1988), the Schools Act, 1992 and by uncertainty leading up to the 1992 general election. In particular, the new legal provisions for:

- the national curriculum
- open enrolment
- formula funding of schools
- opting out of LEA management
- parental choice
- schools inspection
- compulsory competitive tendering

required LEAs and schools to make significant adjustments to the traditional style of and attitude to local governance. Schools were required to make their way in a pupil number driven quasi market, determined largely by consumer choice and strongly framed by national requirements on, for example, the curriculum. Local professional and electoral leadership and power were to be significantly reduced. At the same time, managerial authority was shifting from the LEA to the school and to the Secretary of State. During our project the prospect of a funding agency taking over many LEA functions was on the horizon but not yet promulgated.

Across our three LEAs the consequent shifts in the balance of local control varied significantly. In Hertfordshire, maximisation of parental choice was a long established policy which pre-dated ERA and was expressed, for example, in the absence of distance from school as an admissions criterion. The dominant value emphasised was individual (parental) choice; the consequent need was to facilitate choice and the function was to encourage competition and shared responsibility. The dominant mode of operation was characterised as maximising delegation and restricting intervention, offset by more extensive self conscious emphasis of irreducible services to schools than in other areas including:

building shared values, supporting head teachers, identifying good practice, specialist provision, coordinating new initiatives and interpretation of local needs within the LEA.

In Warwickshire, by contrast, there was an emphasis, more recently promoted than that of Hertfordshire, on systems to complement and balance professional/electoral values. The dominant characteristic in relation to need was increasingly systematic assessment and interpretation of needs, whilst functions emphasised included specifying core activities, providing business services, regulating systems and broking the market. Distinctive Warwickshire modes of operation encompassed limiting market damage to the individual, pursuing the spirit of ERA in terms of delegation, supporting new head-teachers, and being proactive on disciplinary matters.

Coventry offered a different set of emphases again. The predominant values were those of social cohesion; the related wants to be legitimised by elected members were those of the individual and the community. Functions which emerged were tight management of market operation (for example through arranging for client and provider functions to answer to a single officer), evening up provider performance, an honest broker role for individuals and arbitration in cases of difficulty. Distinctive modes of operation included a commitment to a caring style, extensive consultation alongside authoritative decision making and recognition of elected member expertise in terms of locale.

We should make it clear that we are stating emphases here. Elements of all of these values, needs and functions could be found in all three LEAs. There may be an inverse relationship between commitment to delegation and commitment to additional services. The functions emphasised as irreducible in Hertfordshire, the LEA which has valued choice for longest, are more extensive than those emphasised in Warwickshire and in Coventry. In Coventry, emphasis on the needs of the community acts as a counter balance to individual choice and to the needs of schools. This produces the shortest list of irreducible functions, though not necessarily, of course, the shortest list of actual functions.

The apparent discontinuity between willingness to intervene and the range of support provided might derive from the fact that those who do not have such support or who see such support diminishing begin to prize it. It may also have to do with the development curve which follows decisions to delegate. Hertfordshire has a long tradition of non intervention spanning many years prior to the implementation of ERA. It may be that the support role has, in effect, been recreated following wishes from head teachers in the light of non intervention from the authority. War-wickshire has separated very recently the core and business activities it provides for schools and has also started to cost them separately. The variation may reflect reactions to the specific costing and the particular financial difficulties experienced by Warwickshire in the light of the SSA. Finally, Coventry facilitates less delegation in its implementation of ERA and, because of its emphasis on the needs of all three groups, provides support and direction in an homogenous rather than separately identified way. Heads and other users have less information about costs and opportunity costs and less cause to identify separately the need for forms of support which have always existed.

Some of the differences also stem from material differences in the circumstances of each of the authorities. For example, Coventry partici-pants spoke frequently about the virtues of the size, shape and history of Coventry as factors which created a single unified community. In War-wickshire there was a great deal of evidence about the disparity in terms of size, population, wealth and culture of different parts of the Authority's area. Some of this differentiation existed in Hertfordshire also.

Post-ERA approaches to values, needs, functions and modalities
We now summarise the range of approaches in the three LEAs in abstract form, in order to set the context for our fieldwork, alongside our projec-tions and critique. It should be noted, however, that the summary, whilst providing critique and facilitating comparison, risks over simplification; it may suggest rigidity and coherence where reality comprised wide ranging and incremental attempts to integrate new and traditional models of governance.

Values newly emphasised: Individual choice, institutional autonomy, de-ference to nationally determined standards of excellence through inspec-tion, testing and nationally prescribed curricula.

Needs newly emphasised: Informational needs of parents and pupils enab-ling them to select schools where choice exists, national needs for a specific curriculum, national and parental needs for performance infor-mation, institutional need to be freed from interference.

Newly interpreted functions to be provided beyond school level: Administration of government prescribed resource framework, setting local marginal resource frameworks, ensuring sufficient places, monitoring outcomes of educational system, provision of special needs, backup for guarantees, specifying contracts for collectively tendered services.

Needs or functions increasingly discounted: Local variation, equity, choices of forms of quality assurance (e.g. self-evaluation), detailed intervention, specification or purchase of local education provision.

Modes of operation: Delegation to schools predominantly independent of local education authorities and central government prescription of processes such as compulsory competitive tendering, formula funding.

SUMMARY

Our fieldwork has provided us with: a grounding in practical issues perceived by those charged with governing the education system at the time; primary data on educational needs, functions and modes of operation, and secondary data on values; an illustration of education governance in its application post-ERA. These are the base for testing conjectural models. In effect, we have used our fieldwork data to test and interrogate the models which are being developed *a priori* by policy makers. It is to these models that we now turn in Chapter 4.

Models of Educational Governance

We turn now to discussion of the models of educational governance briefly described in Chapter 1. The models we have selected are intended to display the range of thinking about educational governance. Some are already in operation whilst others form part of current discussion, and might appear as proposals over the next decade. We also note some recent examples of patterns of governance.

THE NATURE OF THE MODELS

Models of this kind are intended to be no more than representational devices which bring together and simplify leading elements of complex states. To some extent they are ideal types since in practice none appears in all of its characteristics. Substantial variants of each of them are possible. For example, the professional-electoral model (PE) (see below) could operate if LEAs provided services specified by professionals and provided through managerial systems under the ultimate political control of councillors (as has hitherto been the case). But the traditional mechanisms could be replaced by professionals under political control assessing needs and then purchasing what is needed. This might indeed call for new forms of professional and political behaviour. The model of governance would remain professional-electoral in type.

The utility and force of these models are affected by the historical and geographical contexts in which they operate. Thus a small city area might have developed a political culture in which political and professional networks and belief in public utility are strong. Such an area is more likely to advocate a form of professional-electoral model than would a widely diffused educational system in a large county where networks are more difficult to sustain and the sense of a single polity less accepted.

CONTENTS OF THE MODELS

Each of our models contains the following elements. They are specified in more detail in succeeding chapters:

- values assumed
- needs to be met
- functions to be performed
- modes of operation.

These elements can be used as criteria by which the utility of the models can be judged. The analysis which follows in Chapters 5, 6 and 7 will show the extent to which each model pays attention to different values, needs and functions. Other criteria could concern the extent to which they are workable; we examine these in Chapter 8. For now we attempt to describe each model in terms of their apparent intentions.

THE RANGE OF MODELS

The range of models is shown in Figure 4.1.

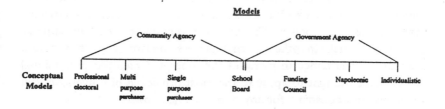

Community Agencies – elected – accountable directly to the local public and the
    Government
Government Agencies – appointed – accountable to local public only though central
    government

Figure 4.1 The range of models of education governance

COMMUNITY AGENCIES

Community agencies are accountable directly to local electorates and have sufficient power to vire funds to ensure that that accountability is realistic.

Professional-electoral (PE)

In the professional-electoral model, power is shared between the head and teachers in the schools and the professional leadership of the authority, with strategic and representative rather than managerial participation by the elected system.

The providers in the schools are largely able to determine the services offered, needs met, and services received by clients. In effect, the professional inputs which determine services offered and needs met are tempered by democratic controls.

It is associated with value positions such as equality (in all its nuances), professionalism, social cohesion and altruism. Its reliance on deficiency funding provides a framework in which the quest for efficiency could be regarded as a second priority.

A professional model?

Within the PE model the power of professionals is likely to be strong. But professionals can exert as much power within other models of governance. For example, the individualistic model allows for clients to exercise their choices within market or quasi-market conditions. The providers, however, might then work within a market of client choices but do so from a base of professional power. The same could apply to the single purpose purchaser model. In other words, professionalism may be a potent element of governance in many of the models. Unalloyed professional models were thought to apply to the most privileged of universities but are an unlikely construct for any public service now.

Multi-purpose public purchaser (MPP)

This model assumes an elected authority mandated by law to perform functions not only in education but also in such adjacent areas as social services. It need not retain a separate committee and structure for education. It is under elected control because of its multi-service remit and its value base in social cohesion, but the emphasis is not on providing services. Its main functions are to assess needs, holistically and systematically, to create contractual arrangements through which the resulting services are purchased from providers separate from themselves, and to evaluate and monitor the extent to which contracting providers are meeting the needs.

Because elected and providing a wide range of services, it is thus capable of sustaining multiple values such as deference to democratic control, the support of social cohesion and the altruistic assumptions of professionalism, but it rests on the mechanism of the purchaser specifying for quality, quantity and price and upon resulting performance.

The purchasing system is intended to ensure that schools and other providers 'deliver' what the clients need, and that the cost is counted. It assumes maximum delegation to schools to ensure that they have sufficient power to meet contractual obligations – it is thus, for example, consistent with local management of schools (LMS). The purchaser would relate to clients through needs assessment and through giving a public account of its actions. The provider would relate closely to clients through interpreting contracts in the light of client wants and experience.

Single purpose public purchaser (SPP)

The single purpose public purchaser model would be exclusively concerned with education but would otherwise be similar to the MPP model described above. It would lay less emphasis on connection between services and might therefore place more emphasis on professional expertise. An important example would be modelled on the NHS district health authority which, as with the SPP, no longer provides but purchases services from providers separated from itself. Because prioritisation and coordination between education and other services are not involved, there is less pressure for an elected local board; indeed, DHAs are not elected.

Individual school board (community agency)

The individual school board (CA) would be concerned with organising and accounting for all internal aspects of delivery of teaching and learning and for all aspects of relationships between the school and external agencies. The only authority beyond the board would be central government although this might establish regional agencies for administrative purposes. The board would be free to purchase services from any provider and to cluster together with other schools for purchasing, for example, insurance or inspecting. The individual school board would, however, be required by statute to be elected and accountable to the local community it serves, and would thus have legitimate authority beyond that conferred by central government.

The justification for this model stems from a range of values of assumptions about needs and mechanisms. For example, it might be run in combination with an individualistic approach (see below) in order to expose schools to the rigour of parental choice. Or it might be adopted as a means of developing a strong professional base.

This model, as with the individualistic model, creates tension around the requirements of ensuring that there are sufficient places and that pupils are educated. Who would ensure that pupils do not fall between school boards? If central government, it must have the power to compel schools to admit pupils; in doing so, it challenges the autonomy of the board.

GOVERNMENT AGENCIES

Government agencies are appointed by and accountable to central government and account to local communities only through central government. Thus the extent of their powers depends upon specific central government choices.

Individual school board (government agency)

This model would be identical to the individual school board (CA) except that it would comprise executive and non executive directors appointed by central government and it would carry no obligation to account to local communities.

The assumption would be that the board's business is management of centrally determined systems in immediate localities. Local community needs would be expressed through choice of school and success against any other performance indicators determined by central government which have local relevance. All of the legitimacy of the board would be conferred by central government which could decide to intervene at will.

Funding councils (FC)

These are appointed by central government and may or may not operate in part through regional or local agencies. They provide funds to institutions which meet their contracts for quality, cost and volume. They thus have the power of purchase and of monitoring associated with it. The determination of contract specification will require some needs assessment and compliance monitoring. They also have power of provision, should they wish to undertake this.

Funding councils differ from SPPs because they are not electorally accountable, because they are not wedded to a particular model of separating purchase and provision, and they are unlikely to sponsor such values as social cohesion. They differ from both the PE and the MPP models because they would not sponsor connection between services. They differ from the proposal in the Education Bill (1992) because they allow a rather fuller model of intervention than that asserted for the funding agency, although it is not unknown for public bodies to grow in assertiveness.

Their leading values would be the pursuit of efficiency and economic growth and maintenance.

Napoleonic (direct central government) (N)

A napoleonic model would assume that the selection of values, the choice of needs to be met, and the functions to be performed would be determined by central government.

This model already substantially applies to the curriculum.

Individualistic client (IC)

Individualistic forms of governance can apply to either the individual client having free rein to purchase from providers, or to a system of individualistic providers able to seek services at a price from a range of providers as in the individual school board model. A full individualistic model would allow for a conjunction of the two.

The individualistic client model could, in theory, form part of any of the preceding models, other than in the professional-electoral or the napoleonic models. Clients backed by public statements of rights, charters or vouchers enabling them to participate in the priced or quasi market could seek services from providers under contract to either of the public purchasers depicted above. But client choices would be constrained by the results of the public purchasers' needs analysis and provision could only partially be driven by an aggregate of largely untreated individual choices. The exercise of choice would be funded by either central government or a funding council acting on its behalf.

The procession of models

In the text we seek to differentiate between the elements of the model and its historical application which varied greatly over forty years. We can discern three periods of governance since the passage of the 1944 Act. The professional-electoral model was dominant following the 1944 Education Act and interpreted locally from then until the legislation of 1988. During that time LEAs were unequivocally providers.

The relative power of the elected member and the professional changed greatly during this period. The power of the professional was thought to be complemented by that of senior councillors and to constitute a 'joint elite' until the 1980s when councillor power became predominant in many authorities.

At the time of our interviews (early 1992), the transitional stage in which many LEAs and institutions found themselves was evident. Many features of the PE model still prevailed, and although each LEA could conceive a further dismantling of the post-1945 system many aspects of the model were seen as highly desirable.

From 1988 onwards, no clear model has been universally in operation. Ingredients of the MPP model were beginning to emerge; the central theme was retention of electoral control as far as that was allowed, whilst attempts were made to take up the purchaser role by LEAs, but this was severely constrained by government rules. The 1988 Act and its associated circulars assumed that for the most part schools would make their way in a pupil number driven market determined largely by consumer choice but strongly framed by national requirements on e.g. the national curriculum and pupil testing. Professional power and leadership were to be at a minimum. The Act left a trail of uncertainty about the role of LEAs which were left with responsibilities to ensure that functions were fulfilled but with weak powers over distribution of resources, over planning and quality assurance.

The 1992 White Paper (see pages 42–43 for details) has removed some of the uncertainty since it leads explicitly to the abandonment of the PE model, except in respect of very limited provider and monitoring functions. It aims to substitute the funding agency for the PE model. Within this, it seems likely that schools will be expected to act largely in an individualistic fashion, and thus follow the example of NHS GP fundholders who are able to purchase treatments from providers such as hospitals. They can take their money where they wish, and the resulting services offered by providers could result from purchasers' demands. As can be seen the White Paper encompasses a range of values and mechanisms which do not amount to a single model; rather they comprise a series of loosely coupled solutions to disparate problems.

Cross model comparison

Each of the models represents a compromise between two dimensions; source and variable degrees of control and approach to delivery. The dimensions and their four poles – central or community authority and purchasing or provision are represented in Figure 4.2. The compromise made by each model is illustrated by the location of the model on the grid.

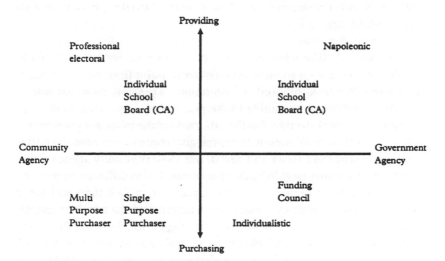

Figure 4.2 Location of models of governance

The vertical dimension of the matrix spans the extent to which models allow for provisions of services at one end of the spectrum, and the extent to which authorities act as purchasers at the other.

There is a wide range of purchasing related models which fall into both the community and government agency sides of the matrix. Purchasing, an approach gaining some acceptability, cannot be associated automatically with the concept of a market. In none of these models is there a freely priced market in which buyers and sellers seek to maximise personal advantage. There are buyers and sellers, but they are not spending their own money and are working within budgetary and other constraints ultimately set by a public or governmental authority. It is true that survival might depend on the success with which providers make available their services but neither the profits nor losses nor the mechanisms of transaction are exactly the same as those of a free market. The essence of the purchaser model is, in fact, that cost and quality are prespecified by a purchaser who then will engage in market style activities in expecting providers to compete with each other. This may create uncertainty in the expectations of the providers but the constraints embodied in the contracting system will tend to dampen the unintended consequences of the market. It is a constrained or social or rigged market. It is a strongly brokered market, calling on skills well beyond those of a market maker in a freely priced market.

The second dimension concerns the source of control. All of our models of governance assume some reference point from which authority is derived. We have referred to community agencies; these are bodies which are directly accountable to the public they serve, usually through some form of local election. On the other side of the range are government agencies, accountable directly to central government, to whom the public must represent their views and needs. But the community agencies, too, exist within a frame established and controlled, if to different degrees, by the centre. Except in the case of the napoleonic model, there will ensue a relationship between the central government and the provider and the purchaser operating in the field. Over the long period that there have been local authorities, the degree of central control has changed several times.

Our models separate distinctive elements of different approaches for the purpose of highlighting their impact and that of different configurations. Grasping the full implications of these models, which make compromises across complex, overlapping issues, requires systematic analysis across the conceptual frameworks, of values, needs or functions.

THE WHITE PAPER – *CHOICE AND DIVERSITY*

The 1992 model is represented, as we write, by the White Paper *Choice and Diversity. A New Framework for Schools* (CM2021, July 1992). The White Paper claims to enhance parental choice by simplifying the creation of grant maintained schools and by opening the way to greater variety through the formation of new schools. The key elements of the White Paper are:

- It establishes the long term funding of grant maintained schools and enables small schools to benefit from Grant Maintained (GM) status.
- It allows new education associations 'to step in to revive declining schools where local authorities or the governors have failed them'.
- It creates a new statutory body for the funding of agencies for schools which will take over from the Department For

Education (DFE) the payment of recurrent and capital grant to GM schools. .

- The funding agency will share with the LEA the duty to secure sufficient secondary or primary school places in the area, from the point where 10% of pupils in the LEA are in GM schools. The funding agency will take over this duty wholly when 75% of pupils are in GM schools 'though the LEA may apply to be relieved of this responsibility well before that point is reached'.

- The Secretary of State will take powers to replace first governors in a GM school where the governing body is failing the school.

- The funding agency for schools and LEAs will have a duty to review the supply of places and to report annually to the Secretary of State. They will both have powers to propose the rationalisation of schools and they may be directed to publish proposals to rationalise schools. The Secretary of State may also publish proposals to rationalise places.

- Until the 75% exit point is reached, LEAs will be able to propose the establishment, closure, significant enlargement or change of schools. .

- LEAs will have final responsibility to ensure that all children attend school or are otherwise suitably educated. They will have a reserve power to direct any LEA maintained or GM school to take a pupil who has not found a place.

Essentially, the White Paper is intended to cause the LEA as a significant entity to wither away. At the same time, the White Paper assumes some type of continuing function for a local authority. It will retain certain responsibilities for all pupils in its area: for special education and state-menting, and for certain other pupil specific support services. It may continue to be responsible for maintaining schools if parents decide not to vote for GM status.

Further constitutional changes include the removal of the requirement to establish an education committee.

An LEA will not be permitted to retain staff and operate any services which go beyond what it requires for the efficient exercise of its own functions within its own area. LEAs may only trade at the margin of capacity. The Government expects that increasingly the private sector will step in to provide some services.

CHAPTER 5

Values

The importance of values and their potential contribution to the analysis of different forms of governance have been described in Chapter 1. We first of all identify the values thought to operate in the domain of education before determining their presence in different models of governance. Our selection is based on published accounts of the nature of values and of governance, and deduction from the needs and functions identified in our fieldwork. This indirect analysis has been necessary because values create dispositions which shape our attitudes to particular organisational forms, tasks and actions rather than explicit, readily observable prescriptions.

Do the reforms of the late 1980s and the 1990s introduce new values? We have not included the market as a value, notwithstanding the tendency of some to assert the importance of the market as a good itself. This is because their arguments relate to operational characteristics. Instead, significant changes in values in relation to the market are considered as second order elements of individuality or social cohesion or excellence.

VALUES PRESENT IN EDUCATION GOVERNANCE

Individuality

Education is committed to developing pupil potential. This leads to an emphasis on the value and nature of the individual. Defences or accounts of the professional-electoral approach to governance, particularly those that give pride of place to professionals' altruistic regard to their clients (for example, the Plowden report on primary education, 1967), imply the importance of unique individuality and this in its turn justifies the autonomy of the teacher and the school, because they then need freedom to create the curriculum in response to individual pupils' needs and wants.

A value may be placed on promoting the rights and life of the individual above other considerations; and from this stem second order consequences such as individual choice of school or the curriculum. Other aspects of individuality are promoted. For example, human nature may be held to be more or less constant over time, or capable of improvement – a fallen angel or noble savage.

Social cohesion

Social cohesion asserts, as a value, connection between individuals and organisations, and the pursuit of community issues. Often it takes forms which are in conflict with the value of the individual, whose proponents would maintain that orientation towards social cohesion diminishes a concern for the individual or at least for individual choice. Mrs Thatcher, for example, declared that there was no such thing as society. Others believe that the two values can complement each other; the empowered individual contributes more to social cohesion, and social cohesion in turn empowers individuals.

Participation

There are degrees of participation (Arnstein, 1969) ranging from merely informing those affected by decisions to sharing decisions, through partnership, and between those mandated to act by election and those who will feel the impact. Participation emphasises elements of other basic values. It respects individual rights to express opinions and wants, and it appeals to social cohesion. Participation is often asserted as a second order, processual, value necessary for social cohesion. As in the case of the rights of the individual, 'in its extreme form the argument for participation as a value in local government is rooted in the primacy of the community... It is possible, though not always easy, to define over most of the country self conscious communities and to argue that their citizens should have some mechanism for promoting or protecting their collective interests.' (Sharpe, 1970, p.160). Proponents of individual choice would claim that aggregated individual choices do, in fact, constitute participation, even though they might not advance participation as a value. But the absence of social cohesion would be thought by some to diminish the commitment to participation.

Equality

In education, as in other public services, equality separates into two potentially conflicting value sets. The soft or weak versions (in Anthony Crosland's term) offer equality of opportunity. In the allocation and distribution of resources the weak version emphasises equality of input rather than outcome as if that would sufficiently guarantee social justice. This value might restrict equality to offering the same opportunity of choosing a school to all parents. Such equality would be underpinned by charters restricted to the process of expressing and hearing the preference. In the hard or strong version there would be a commitment to ensuring equality of output underpinned through the allocation of resource and commitment to actions to redress disadvantage. The resource required would be determined on the basis of what is needed to raise performance from the entry point of individuals to an agreed norm.

Economic strength

There has always been ambivalence about the advancement of economic strength as an educational value. There are soft and hard versions of this value. In the hard version, education would be concerned with providing the specific skills and attributes required by a strong economy. In the soft version education would be concerned with the development of the whole person in order that individuals can contribute to collective economic health. In this view education and economic strength should be only loosely coupled, to ensure a liberal education and to avoid risks of exploitation.

Excellence

Excellence is a value motivating several of the emerging models of governance. It assumes that individual competencies in defined skills and knowledge are a supreme objective even if it places equality and social cohesion at a discount. Excellence takes up selected aspects of the individuality value. It may be advanced as contributing not only to individual worth but also as a contribution to social development through its production of individuals who will make exemplary contributions to economic growth and maintenance. Alternative views would maintain that excellence should be defined by the circumstances of pupils which might allow for other objectives than defined skills and knowledge.

Altruism

Altruism embodies concern for others and has been a value dominant in the post-1945 professional electoral model of educational governance, in which professional officers and elected members are expected to act for the good of, and on behalf of, others.

Equity

Equity, to be distinguished from equality, is the value of agreeing and abiding by rules and mechanisms through which governance and the distribution of resource take place. It appeals to the morality of ensuring that all will be subject to the even handed application of rules. It is a value prominently manifested in bureaucratic modes of governance and takes a weaker form in market modes since market forces are in themselves a substitute for government criteria, decision and judgement.

Efficiency

Efficiency, whilst frequently asserted as a self evident good, is a means through which other values are realised and/or tempered. Efficiency entails judgement between price and some other objective or value. It is not an autonomous value and may be in conflict with such values as equity. Its definition has changed in recent decades from a belief in good working together to a belief in value for money.

Democracy

Democratic values are differently expressed but all start with the belief that policies should be mandated by an expression of the popular will, usually through elections.

Because systems of democracy take different forms, democracy is accompanied by a wide range of associated values which are revealed in the forms of democracy taken in our models of governance. Some versions endorse remote and 'ballot box' democracy (for example, funding councils) and others proximate and participative democracy (professional-electoral and multi-purpose purchaser).

Professionalism

Professionalism is defined as embodying an altruistic regard for the needs of clients and the use of esoteric knowledge on their behalf. In Chapter

8 we will explore the extent to which new patterns of governance call for the development of new forms of professionalism.

VALUE EMPHASIS IN DIFFERENT GOVERNMENT MODELS

In the analysis which follows, the judgements made are explicitly stated. They have been checked against:

- our interpretation of models of governance which encompass different value stances
- needs, functions and modes of operation emerging from the fieldwork
- the needs, functions and modes of operation evident across our models
- discussions of these issues in current policy literature
- current statutes.

To expose our own thinking we have identified the value emphasis we perceive to be implied by each model on a score between 1 and 5 (Table 5.1). A score of 1 indicates that we discern clear discounting of a value within the model. A score of 3 indicates a modest orientation towards a value, and a score of 5 denotes of a heavy emphasis of a value in the nature of the model.

We have tried in each case to construe the model as it is advocated rather than to assess whether intentions are likely to be matched by outcomes. We have used scoring of 4 and 2 only where they are necessary to illustrate distinctions between the approaches of the different models. We do not imply that a score of 5 is better than a score of 1. Nor do we imply that these figures flow from quantitative research.

We have also used this scoring to identify crucial components of historical and currently proposed systems of governance, in order to compare the conceptual models described in Chapter 4 with the patterns actually at work, or contemplated for future working, in the post-1945 period, in the period between ERA (1988) and the 1992 White Paper and in the post-1992 period.

In the text which follows the charts we have illustrated the questions raised by this approach and the use to which it might be put. We suggest that policy players might work through a similar analysis for themselves. Although our perceptions of the weight of the different values in each model are inevitably coloured by our own values, we have used informed discussions with others to test our thinking.

Table 5.1 Values endorsed in different models

	CONCEPTUAL MODELS						HISTORICAL APPLICATION	
	COMMUNITY AGENCIES			GOVERNMENT AGENCIES			Post-1945	White Paper
	Professional electoral	Single Purpose Purchaser	Multi Purpose Purchaser	Individual School Board (CA)	Individual School Board (GA)	Funding Council	Individualistic		
Individuality	3	4	3	3	3	3	5	3	4
Social cohesion	4	2	4	2	1	1	1	4	2
Economic strength	3	4	3	3	3	5	3	2	4
Equality	4	3	4	3	2	3	1	4	2
Equity	3	3	4	2	2	4	1	4	2
Altruism	4	3	4	4	3	2	1	5	2
Efficiency	3	4	3	3	3	5	3	1	4
Democracy	5	1	4	3	1	1	1	4	2
Participation	5	2	4	2	1	1	3	3	2
Professionalism	4	4	3	5	4	2	1	5	2
Public Accountability	5	2	4	3	2	1	1	4	2
Excellence	3	3	2	3	3	3	5	2	3

To illustrate the purpose and outcome of this tabulation we take up two particular values in detail, namely, individual choice and social cohesion:

Individual Choice

Table 5.2 Individual choice

	Professional electoral	Single Purpose Purchaser	Multi Purpose Purxhaser	Individual School Board (CA)	Individual School Board (GA)	Funding Council	Individualistic	Post-1945	White Paper
Individuality	3	4	3	3	3	3	5	3	3–4

A professional-electoral model would neither emphasise nor discount individual choice but would not give this value high priority. Nor would the single purpose purchaser, multi-purpose purchaser, individual school board or the funding council models.

But beyond these broad similarities (expressed as scores between 3 and 4) there are important distinctions:

- The purchaser models would emphasise individuality through holistic studies of needs, as well as through allowing providers to maximise choice.

- But the multi-purpose purchaser would have to balance the value of individuality against multiple public responsibilities and hence is scored as 3.

- The funding council would be more dependent upon fluctuations in the values of central government, to which it is answerable, with even wider ranging public responsibilities (for the economy, health, defence, etc).

- The individual school board models would allow for individuality by locating decision making near to individuals but would also make possible a strongly provider driven system unless surplus places were maintained to ensure that school competition for pupils increased potential 'purchasing power'.

- The individualistic model would most obviously place the utmost emphasis on individual choice.

Social cohesion

Table 5.3 Social cohesion

	Professional electoral	Single Purpose Purchaser	Multi Purpose Purchaser	Individual School Board (CA)	Individual School Board (GA)	Funding Council	Individualistic	Post 1945	White Paper
Social cohesion	4	2	4	2	1	1	1	4	2

A disposition towards social cohesion, stability and local communities would be a feature of a professional-electoral model, in which the entity is accountable to a local community. A multi-purpose purchasing model would also place high emphasis on such values, but its commitment to a purchaser/ provider mechanism would mean that values of social cohesion were tempered by an increased emphasis on efficiency and constrained by the separation of direct provision from purchasing.

The distinctions between the various models comprise:

- The single purpose purchaser, by governing education as a single, isolated public service would discount social cohesion.

- The funding council and individualistic models would discount social cohesion, but from rather different standpoints. Like the single purpose purchaser, the funding council would discount social cohesion because it separates education from other community services. Its capacity to take a cohesive overview would be directed more towards a national overview of education than towards community cohesion. Beyond this, a funding council could either provide or de-emphasise such values within its overall remit, but its probable commitment to non intervention would make such promotion uncertain. (Nonetheless we felt the scoring here was ambiguous and could equally have indicated a score of 2 for the funding council).

- The discounting of social cohesion for an individualistic model is self evident, although some proponents of such models might believe that participation through individual choice and aggregation of individual choice can lead to social cohesion. Such a view does not imply a value emphasis; it is rather a question of a preferred mode of operation.

- The post-1945 LEA emphasised social cohesion through its multi-purpose and democratic remit.

- The White Paper discounts social cohesion, by emphasising diversity and choice.

- Individual school boards as models also discount social cohesion since, like the other single purpose model, they focuses only upon education, even though some boards may try to emphasise social cohesion; the community agency individual school board will emphasise social cohesion slightly more that its government agency counterpart through its local elected base and accountability.

AMBIVALENCES IN RATINGS

The importance and complexity of values can also be illustrated by some of the tensions brought about by attempting sharp differentiation.

One might expect that the post-1945 and White Paper applications of governance would adopt sharply differentiated approaches to individuality. We think not. Whilst the historical application of the professional-electoral pattern is often criticised as unable to facilitate individual choice because it pursues equality and community values, it also emphasises individualised learning as construed by professionals, expressed, for example, through a reluctance to publish individual performance norms. Individual choice is sponsored in professional-electoral models (including the community individual school board) but related more to the curriculum and learning processes than to institutions. In the Education Reform Act, 1988 individual choice of institution was given more rein than in the 1992 White Paper, since the latter proposes new powers to close schools, which will certainly constrain individual choice.

Can a commitment to the value of social cohesion be deduced from the White Paper provisions on planning? We think not. First, the White Paper and subsequent ministerial interpretation emphasise that although the funding agency and Secretary of State are to have new, stronger powers on school closure, these will not amount to planning. Second, whilst the removal of significant LEA powers will happen incrementally, triggered by an aggregation of parental ballots for individual schools, and is an electoral process, it does not involve whole electorates and those who vote cannot then vote on a change of mind. This is not diversity from the centre to allow local groups to pursue local social cohesion; it is diversity pursued as an end in itself. For example, whilst the White Paper implies that constrained cohesion amongst grant-maintained schools might be allowed through clusters, it makes no provisions to encourage it.

There are complexities inherent in the scorings for the value of equality. Proponents of the individualistic model could argue that a focus on individual choice and aggregated choice emphasises equality of treatment. But emphasising equality of treatment implies subordinating individual choice to public planning for equal provision and so a score of 1 has been allocated. Proponents of the White Paper might, with justification, also argue that the provisions for special needs and for compelling schools to admit pupils allow for an emphasis on equality. The low scoring reflects, however, the fact that choice, (the target of the provisions), is not only not equally available, (since school places are not equally available), but also the fact that the Paper proposes strong measures to remove surplus places, thus making choice differentially available. It should be noted that in general scoring the White Paper in this way is problematic because it is not in fact a model but a series of discrete propositions and policies brought together at a particular point in time. It therefore pursues multiple, contradictory values and hence needs and functions.

RELATIVE EMPHASIS BETWEEN VALUES

Altruism

Table 5.4 Altruism

	Professional electoral	Single Purpose Purchaser	Multi Purpose Purchaser	Individual School Board (CA)	Individual School Board (GA)	Funding Council	Individualistic	Post-1945	White Paper
Altruism	4	3	4	4	3	2	1	5	2

Interesting tensions emerge from the different interpretations of values adopted in different models. We take altruism first:

- The multi-purpose purchaser model assumes that individuals need coherent public services and that they are unable to achieve coherence between large public services themselves; altruism is therefore emphasised by making connections on the individuals' behalf.

- A single purpose purchaser and the multi-purpose purchaser emphasise altruism through taking needs analysis as the baseline for specifying services.

- The professional-electoral model, by contrast, assumes that professionals will be committed to altruism and that professional expertise and democratic accountability are necessary if individual rights are to be fulfilled. It is the exercise of such 'on behalfist' judgements that spawned a reinterpretation of individuality. In new proposals individuality has moved from endorsing individual need to endorsing individual choice, interpretations which pull in opposite directions.

Efficiency

Table 5.5 Efficiency

	Professional electoral	Single Purpose Purchaser	Multi Purpose Purxhaser	Individual School Board (CA)	Individual School Board (GA)	Funding Council	Individualistic	Post 1945	White Paper
Efficiency	3	4	3	3	3	5	3	1	4

Historically, deficiency funding allowed for discounting of efficiency as it is now understood. Beyond this base line, scoring of this value for our conceptual models reflects the extent to which they are likely to subordinate efficiency to other values; that is, these scores have a direct relationship with the strength of emphasis given to other values. For example, the single purpose models are freer to concentrate on educational efficiency because of their narrower remit. The White Paper introduces specific measures to increase efficiency in terms of surplus places but at the same time it allows for dual regulation of the system through funding agencies and LEAs, a patent discounting of the efficiency value, and therefore we ascribe a relatively neutral score of 3.

Democracy

Table 5.6 Democracy

	Professional electoral	Single Purpose Purchaser	Multi Purpose Purxhaser	Individual School Board (CA)	Individual School Board (GA)	Funding Council	Individualistic	Post 1945	White Paper
Democracy	5	1	4	3	1	1	1	4	2

There are several forms of democracy. One distinction is between formal or ballot box democracy and participative democracy. Another distinction is between remote and proximate democracy. The professional-electoral model should in principle be both participative and proximate although historically neither the professionals nor the elected leaders have always been willing or competent to ensure participation in and testing of their work by clients. The funding council, individualistic and White Paper patterns derive their democratic legitimacy from Parliament. But our scoring reflects the fact that neither the Funding Council nor the individualistic model propound democratic procedures in their ways of determining policy and action. The democracy is disclosed only in their origins which would be determined by parliamentary sanctioned legislation. In their operation they will act as part of a remote democracy, and not directly accountable to elected members.

As far as the White Paper is concerned, the balloting of parents on opting-out and retention of a role for the elected LEA until removed again allow for democratic input at a formative point in time. But these mechanisms do not allow for testing and reiterative legitimising of these arrangements. They allow only for a democratic decision at the inauguration of a new structure and are not dissimilar from electorates being given the right to vote in favour of a one party state or a non-electoral system. Subsequent participation is limited to the exercise of office by the minority of parent governors.

Participation

Table 5.7 Participation

	Professional electoral	Single Purpose Purchaser	Multi Purpose Purchaser	Individual School Board (CA)	Individual School Board (GA)	Funding Council	Individualistic	Post 1945	White Paper
Participation	5	2	4	2	1	1	3	3	2

This value is shown as being only weakly present in the single purpose purchaser model because the specialist remit of the intermediary entity will emphasise expertise and discourage lay participation. Its stronger presence in the multi-purpose purchasing model is based upon the assumption that strong articulation with other public services invites competition for resources with other local government services and so involves participation across the community and through local democracy.

The participation value would be strongly present in the individualistic model in relation to parents, because choice represents a form of participation. This has, however, to be balanced against the tendency to allow for participation only through the choices of existing parents and pupils as opposed to participation of other stakeholders such as employers, community groups, school neighbours and future parents and pupils.

Proponents of the traditional post-1945 model may consider that participation has been more strongly emphasised than 3. The score is limited to 3 because future models all contain the possibility of incorporating new participative mechanisms including, for example, polling of consumer perceptions to complement previous approaches.

Professionalism

Table 5.8 Professionalism

	Professional electoral	Single Purpose Purchaser	Multi Purpose Purchaser	Individual School Board (CA)	Individual School Board (GA)	Funding Council	Individualistic	Post 1945	White Paper
Professionalism	4	4	3	5	4	2	1	5	2

Within the purchaser models the single purpose model is seen to emphasise professionalism more than the multi purpose authority because, in the latter, professional interpretation of assessment of need, of specifications and delivery will be tempered by similar judgements about other connected services and also, to some degree by judgements of elected officials.

Our scoring reflects puzzling differences in the post-1945 approach. Why should professionalism be scored at 5, if democracy is only 4? Our thinking is that despite increasing intervention from elected members, the model was strongly professional and that LEA intervention in the curriculum remained relatively weak, especially if this is compared with the National Curriculum.

Public Accountability

Table 5.9 Accountability

	Professional electoral	Single Purpose Purchaser	Multi Purpose Purxhaser	Individual School Board (CA)	Individual School Board (GA)	Funding Council	Individualistic	Post 1945	White Paper
Accountability	5	2	4	3	2	1	1	4	2

The government agency models present a limited emphasis on public accountability since they operate through ministers and their departments. Such models are not based on direct accountability to those to whom the service is provided. However, unless the single purpose purchasing model is specifically constructed for it, it may not emphasise public accountability, as in the case of district health authorities.

Excellence

Table 5.10 Excellence

	Professional electoral	Single Purpose Purchaser	Multi Purpose Purxhaser	Individual School Board (CA)	Individual School Board (GA)	Funding Council	Individualistic	Post 1945	White Paper
Excellence	3	3	2	3	3	3	5	2	3

It is hard to envisage any model totally discounting excellence. It is the relative emphasis on excellence in the individualistic model which is revealing: other models may emphasise excellence over, say, efficiency or equality. The attribution of a score of 5 to the individualistic model's treatment of excellence denotes the commitment in this model to the ability of market forces to produce excellence through competition. Even for those who accept this argument, however, the emphasis would imply the removal of the main constraints on the education market – compulsory attendance and statutory provision for all which are strongly endorsed in the public agency models.

We hope that we have shown both the implications and usefulness of this means of comparing values and models. In illustrating our thinking our aim is to prompt others to attempt similar analyses as well as to inform; there is no single, 'correct' score which can be ascribed. Figure 5.1 presents four basic values as bar charts as a means of illustrating patterns and emphasis. In this format the significant variation between models is self evident, as is the fact that the professional-electoral and multi purpose purchaser models are more intensely value driven than others. From a values perspective the White Paper application appears to have much in common with the individualistic model. Similarly the professional electoral and multi purpose purchasing models align closely in the frame. But similarity between values does not imply consonance in terms of needs, functions and modes of operation, as will be shown in subsequent chapters.

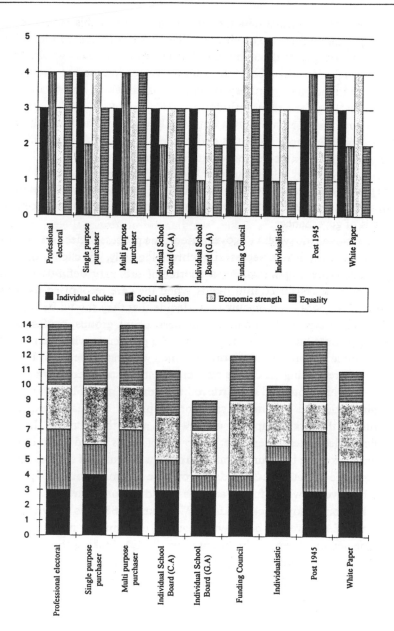

Figure 5.1 Values analysis

CHAPTER 6

Needs

The purpose of this chapter is to examine the nature of educational needs and to identify them in ways which allow for comparison between the models of governance.

In a rationalistic system of government, the process of needs definition begins logically, if not necessarily chronologically, by clients or their providers expressing wants. As a matter of arbitrary definition, these wants become converted into needs when they are recognised by those who have authority and resources to decide that they should be met.

Such agencies might include providers, client groups, professionals who contribute the first line of analysis and politicians who then decide the resource allocation and planning which will enable needs to be met. In the nature of things, it can be expected that the statement of wants will be more voluminous and less ordered than that of needs. But wants may remain undefined or unexpressed or be poorly or weakly expressed because of the lack of capacity or power to make them known. In a full public service system, therefore, discovery of wants would be an important initial exercise to be undertaken from a wide range of sources and by a wide range of methods. Such data would be a primary source of policies and objectives to which future actions would be committed.

At least one study (Packwood and Whitaker, 1988), has shown how, in general, LEAs have not been systematic in determining needs analysis, with the notable exception in recent years of LEA thinking about the now separated Further Education (FE) sector. Commonly, LEAs have relied on professional judgments expressed largely in terms of institutional requests for resources as mediated, perhaps, through advisers or inspectors. For example, a sixth form centre might identify growing demands for instruction in Information Technology (IT), or language instruction for students recently arrived in the UK. This 'want' would be stated as a case in terms of courses and other provision being necessary to meet new demands. It might be scrutinised by an adviser before it finds its way in the competition for resources. Then the LEA would make an implicit or explicit judgment of needs which would generally be expressed as resource allocation. Ultimately such judgements are a political process in two senses: the final decisions belong to politicians, and they may involve a process of bargaining – the stuff of politics, rather than of rationalistic planning – as well as a scrutiny of all evidence.

The systematic alternative would be for the education department to start with an assessment of social and employment patterns and of the age and origins of potential clients living in an area, then assess the resulting potential demand for courses in consultation with institutions and advisers and finally reach judgements about a hierarchy of needs. There would also be some attempt to explore the extent of unstated wants in the population.

The optimum elements of holistic needs assessment are thus:
- a systematic set of surveys of individual and community wants
- expression of wants as stated by providers
- a set of more distanced professional judgements
- a political process which takes the resulting data and recommendations and determines priorities and distributions.

Within rational market models, however, the discovery of wants is handled on the basis of the operation and aggregation of individual choice. The market assumes that providers and clients strive to maximise their own utility. The provider seeks to establish what consumers want and to provide it at the price which will attract most consumers. They will then maximise their profits. The consumer seeks to maximise personal advantage by getting the most competent service available at the smallest opportunity cost of convenience and money. The market assumes knowledge on the part of both. It assumes that the consumer knows what education he or she or his or her child wants and needs and how to go about finding, selecting and purchasing it. It assumes that providers know how to find out about consumer wants and how to meet them. In this framework, therefore, the importance of discovering wants is not denied but neither is it facilitated. This alternative way of determining and satisfying needs is proposed as more effective than rational planning, and underpins the individualistic, and to some extent, the purchasing models. We have noted earlier that the market is a contrived version and these mechanisms may not work.

The analysis of needs and wants should, together with the analysis of values, substantiate the critiques to be applied to our models. Do the

Table 6.1 Needs allowed by conceptual models

| | CONCEPTUAL MODELS | | | | | | | HISTORIC APPLICATIONS | |
| | COMMUNITY AGENCY | | | | GOVERNMENT AGENCY | | | Post 1945 | White Paper |
	Professional electoral	Single purpose purchaser	Multi-purpose purchaser	Individual School Board (CA)	Individual School Board (GA)	Funding Council	Individualistic		
Individual Needs									
Educational needs	4	5	4	5	5	5	4	4	4
Parents' information on choice	2	3	2	5	5	2	5	2	4
Place provision	5	5	5	5	5	5	3	5	5
Provision for vulnerable	4	4	4	3	2	3	2	5	3
Quasi-judicial	3	5	5	3	2	3	3	4	3
Special educational needs	5	4	4	3	3	4	2	4	4
Needs of the community									
Employment skills	4	3	4	3	3	3	3	3	3
Specifying standards	3	5	4	3	5	5	4	2	3
Monitoring of specified standards	4	5	4	3	5	5	4	2	3
Democratic representation	3	1	4	3	1	1	1	3	2
Convergence with other public services	5	2	5	2	1	2	1	4	1
Ensuring compliance with statute	3	2	4	3	5	2	3	4	2
Facilitate social cohesion	5	3	4	3	1	1	1	4	1
Convergent prioritisation within education	5	3	3	1	1	3	1	4	3
Financial regulation	3	3	4	4	3	4	3	4	3
Correcting poor performance	5	3	3	1	3	3	1	4	4
Holistic overview	5	3	5	1	1	3	1	4	3
Giving a public account	5	3	4	3	1	2	2	4	3
Resource allocation	4	3	3	3	3	3	2	4	2
Balancing long term & short term needs	5	5	5	2	2	4	1	4	3
Broker/regulator of market	1	5	4	1	1	3	1	1	1

Table 6.1 Needs allowed by conceptual models (continued)

| | CONCEPTUAL MODELS | | | | | | | HISTORIC APPLICATIONS | |
| | COMMUNITY AGENCY | | | GOVERNMENT AGENCY | | | | Post 1945 | White Paper |
	Professional electoral	Single purpose purchaser	Multi-purpose purchaser	Individual School Board (CA)	Individual School Board (GA)	Funding Council	Individualistic		
Providers needs									
Moral & professional leadership	5	3	4	2	2	2	1	4	2
Moral & professional support	4	2	2	1	1	1	1	4	1
Professional discretion	4	3	2	4	4	3	3	4	2
Institutional autonomy	1	4	4	5	5	3	5	2	5
Support for small schools	4	3	3	3	3	2	1	3	1
Insurance against emergencies	5	3	4	1	3	3	1	5	1
Provision of services	5	1	2	1	3	1	1	5	1

models allow and encourage assessment of wants? How do models allow for informing and encouraging the expression of wants which do not fit a norm or past practice? What process will best allow educational providers, and those who set the policy frame for educational provision, to take account of wants as they become recognised as needs?

In addition to needs derived from wants, however, there are statutory requirements which generate needs which may well not be 'wanted'. Those related to compulsory take-up by unwilling clients are the obvious examples. There are, too, new necessities caused by social, economic or technical developments which may not have emerged as educational wants at any given time. For the purpose of comparing models we have also, therefore, amplified our analysis of wants and needs as discussed in our fieldwork with statutory requirements and admonitions.

How do the models outlined in Chapter 1, and elaborated in Chapter 4 meet the needs expressed in our field work interviews and in statute?

Table 6.1 sets out our perceptions which we have exposed in tabular form the relative emphasis allocated to needs by each model.

It should be noted that our statement of needs emphasised or discounted by the models is fuller than our statements of values or functions because we have used it as a means of relating present experience to alternative possibilities. Furthermore, we have separated the needs of the individual, the community and providers since these may be in contention.

As with values we shall illustrate our analysis by describing our interpretation of one or two specific needs for each of the customers of education governance – individual parents and pupils, the community and providers.

Table 6.2 Individual needs – educational needs

	Professional electoral	Single purpose purchaser	Multi-purpose purchaser	Individual School Board (CA)	Individual School Board (GA)	Funding Council	Individualistic	Post 1945	White Paper
Educational needs	4	5	4	5	5	5	4	4	4

All conceptual models of educational governance and all historical or proposed systems must give heavy emphasis to educational needs – providing teaching and enabling learning. Whilst some models will assume that this can best be delivered through maximum delegation to schools and others will assume that such needs require provision by an intermediary body, such variation does not imply a discounting of the need. The only models in which the need might be discounted would be those which balance educational needs against other needs. In each of our three LEA areas and in all models except the single purpose there was a substantial emphasis on ensuring that educational needs vied with, for example, social or housing needs. Thus, the professional-electoral, and the multi purpose purchaser models, together with the post-1945 and post-ERA applications, are given a score of 4 against a score of 5 for the single purpose purchaser, funding council and individual school board models. The individualistic model has also attracted a score of 4 since, in our analysis, that model emphasises the need for individual choice over straightforward educational needs.

It is unlikely that proponents of any model would be comfortable with explicit discounting of the needs of the vulnerable. The proposition tested here, however, is the extent to which the model, by virtue of its composition, automatically emphasises such needs.

Table 6.3 Individual needs – provision for the vulnerable

	Professional electoral	Single purpose purchaser	Multi-purpose purchaser	Individual School Board (CA)	Individual School Board (GA)	Funding Council	Individualistic	Post 1945	White Paper
Provision for the vulnerable	4	4	4	3	2	3	2	5	3

The view reflected by our scoring is that

- The professional-electoral model will attend to such needs through its emphasis on professional values and mechanisms and on electoral representation of the disadvantaged.

- The single and multi purpose purchasing models do so through the emphasis on holistic assessment of needs.

- The individual school board models, however, will emphasise the needs of the school for success, as well as the needs of individuals, and thus de-emphasise the needs of those whose vulnerability threatens school success; this would be particularly true of individual school boards not directly accountable to a local community.

Hence our attribution of a score of 3 for a public agency individual school board and of 2 to an individual school board acting as a government agency.

The individualistic model emphasises individual choice over need, and makes little allowance for the operation of professional intervention to meet expectations. In its pure form this model, in emphasising market forces, would almost certainly remove the duty to provide places for all pupils, since it is this duty which constrains the closure of failing schools freely following the pattern of parental choice. In these circumstances, the needs of vulnerable individuals could easily be passed by for a significant period; hence the score of 1 for this model.

The historic patterns of the welfare state and deficiency funding were clearly evident in our fieldwork, and this is reflected in the post-1945 score of 5, as was recognition of the tension for schools between pursuing their own success and meeting the needs of vulnerable and difficult pupils. The score of 2 against this need for the White Paper is perhaps more ambiguous. The White Paper itself introduces new powers to require GM schools, too, to take individual pupils; on this basis a score of 4 or 5 might seem appropriate. On the other hand, the emphasis on limiting LEA powers to allocate funds for socio economic needs, enhanced funding for GM schools and on a national funding formula all imply a discounting of the individual needs of the vulnerable.

Our questions tested views about the nature of the community in terms of educational governance and about its needs. Broadly the community incorporated under a collective umbrella such wide ranging entities as future parents and pupils, local employers, school neighbours, and local pressure groups including religious organisations.

Table 6.4 Needs of the community – balancing long and short term needs

	Professional electoral	Single purpose purchaser	Multi- purpose purchaser	Individual School Board (CA)	Individual School Board (GA)	Funding Council	Individualistic	Post 1945	White Paper
Balancing long and short term needs	5	5	5	2	2	4	1	4	3

Balancing long and short term needs is a requirement which goes beyond, and might lie in opposition to, the needs of existing individual parents and pupils and providers. It is precisely the kind of need which both professional and elected institutions are assumed to meet; even if, in practice, this might have been a counsel of perfection; hence the attribution of 5. The purchasing models, as described in Chapter 4, emphasise planning and an intrinsic capacity to balance long and short term needs, which we have assessed as 5. The funding council also emphasises planning but gives less attention to systematic needs assessment. This would be limited to broad survey and the expression of needs through schools rather than through the political collection of clients' wants; hence our attribution of 4.

By contrast, both individual school board models generate pressures to emphasise the needs of current parents and pupils above the needs of their future counterparts. This pressure is further exacerbated if market forces are extended as in the individualistic model. LEAs have traditionally emphasised a planning function in their structure although, as noted in our fieldwork, the GM provisions of ERA have pulled practicality and theory in opposite directions; hence the score of 4. The White Paper has made some limited steps towards pre-ERA practice by formally emphasising the importance of planning for school creation and closure.

All three local authority areas in our study identified, in different terms, a need for local management of the 'social market' (see Chapter 3). This will take different forms in different areas but will comprise meeting the collective needs of providers and users for a full range of services (for example, identifying and ensuring the making good of 'gaps' in service provision), anticipation of new and specialist needs, and communication of needs and information to ensure that purchasing and provision are relevant and timely. It is possible to convert such needs into functions such as strategic marketing and/or research and development for groups of schools, for stakeholders and for users.

Table 6.5 Community needs – broker/regulator of market

	Professional electoral	Single purpose purchaser	Multi-purpose purchaser	Individual School Board (CA)	Individual School Board (GA)	Funding Council	Individualistic	Post 1945	White Paper
Broker/ regulator of market	1	5	4	1	1	3	1	1	1

Our models would cope with these needs as follows:
- The professional-electoral model would discount (as presented at a score of 1) such needs in the sense that the model is an

antithesis of the market – although it might attempt to perform many market functions and anticipate some of the needs.

- The single purpose purchaser would give a great deal of attention to this role, because it is based upon a purchasing/provision logic and single purpose span of responsibility.

- The multi-purpose purchaser would share the logical disposition towards the role but would substitute a stronger planning function and democratic processes for market regulation *per se*, to sustain choices between multiple public needs; hence an attributed score of 4.

- Whilst a funding council model would entail a full range of services made available to providers, and would be likely to investigate cases where such a range was not available, it would be unlikely to take on a proactive regulatory role, preferring instead to influence through its relationships with providers and central government.

- By contrast, individual school boards, whilst wishing to see a full range of services, would not easily be able to carry out such a role. It is possible that, for example, clusters or teachers' professional associations might seek a role here but this would be serendipitous, not implied by the model.

- The individualistic model, above all others, would generate a need for 'broking', since it would tend to atomise provision and isolate both schools and those who support them. By the same token, its ideology would oppose regulation, urging instead the operation of as free a market as possible

- The post-1945 version of the professional-electoral model, like its conceptual counterpart, gave no emphasis to market regulation; largely in this case because, as a monopolistic provider, it precluded market conditions.

- Finally, although the White Paper appears to recognise a need for such provision by, for example, allowing clusters which could act as purchasing consortia, it is explicitly committed to an incremental reduction in the LEA or even funding agency intervention.

Surprisingly, a strongly felt need for collective moral and professional leadership of schools emerged even amongst respondents who saw little or no need for support, external inspection or advice. This need was explained as a desire that educational governance should be based on and reflect the positive values which should underpin the education process. It also included concern that some organisation beyond the school should ensure that competition is not allowed to 'level down' the ethical practice of schools with regard, say, to admissions or towards meeting the needs of the disadvantaged who also happen to be disruptive.

Table 6.6 Providers' needs – moral and professional leadership

	Professional electoral	Single purpose purchaser	Multi-purpose purchaser	Individual School Board (GA)	Individual School Board (GA)	Funding Council	Individualistic	Post 1945	White Paper
Moral and professional leadership	5	3	4	1	2	2	1	4	2

Of the models in this domain:

- The professional-electoral model would be most active, since the determination of and response to values are matters central to both democratic and professional structures.

- Both purchasing models would be more reticent, offering only systematic needs assessment and consequent specifications of service as implicit moral and professional leadership, since these models both eschew direct provision; on the other hand both might allow for such leadership implicitly, in their information and market broking roles.

- The multi-purpose model, by advocating the balancing of a range of public services, explicitly espouses a particular value set which might be said to constitute and offer opportunities for such leadership.

- The funding council's position would be similar to that of the single purpose purchaser but would lack the base of multi-level needs assessment.

- Like the funding council, the individual school board models would also discount this need but for different reasons. The isolation of the school within these models would reinforce the absence of an intermediary entity capable of drawing schools together into a local, moral framework. Given the need for a moral and professional frame, individual school boards would no doubt try to fill the vacuum. Their ability to do so would be constrained by the isolation implied by the model and by their dependency upon a non interventionist central government to restrain wayward schools.

- The individualistic model assumes that the operation of aggregated choice is a reliable and appropriate substitute for moral and professional leadership and so the need is discounted.

- Historically, moral and professional leadership was emphasised through partnership between LEA professionals and elected members but the White Paper, whilst espousing the notion of moral leadership for pupils, asserts strongly an intention to ensure that the funding agency takes on no such role at the level of the system.

In a system with finite resources, all needs must compete. For example, the need of a particular school for professional discretion may be in contradiction with the needs of the community for convergence with other services, for a public account or for specific employment skills. Similarly, the needs of a parent for information on choice may contradict school needs for professional discretion. The needs of one pupil for a school place often compete with the needs of another or with the long term needs of the community for places elsewhere. Special needs of one pupil may contend with the needs of other individual pupils. The needs of individual parents may demand that an intermediary entity should overule a school. But at the same time the school will have a need for that intermediary agency to be willing to do its bidding and the intermediary agency is itself dependent upon the school for its survival. The line by line analysis, whilst helpful in enabling comparison, may thus impose a spurious separation on needs which have a dynamic relationship with each other. But the most important separation is between groups of needs; allowance must be made for related but distinct consideration of the needs of our three main groups.

ANOMALIES OR AMBIGUITIES IN NEEDS ASSESSMENT

As in the case of values, our scoring provides a frame for comparison rather than an assertion of a single 'right' analysis. Although we have attempted to create conceptual models sufficiently robust to withstand this kind of testing, there remain ambiguities which serve to illustrate tensions between different approaches for example:

- The White Paper, whilst commending the provision of information to parents on choice, falls short of a total commitment because of its provisions for school closure and the like; we have therefore attributed a score of 4.

- The individualistic model is shown as discounting the need for the provision of places, since for the market to operate effectively to force excellence through competition it would need to be freed from the current requirements for ensuring sufficient places in particular areas.

- The single and multi purpose purchasers are shown as emphasising quasi judicial needs more strongly than the professional-electoral model because their judgement is freed from the interests of providers since they are not themselves providers, but purchasers. The funding council, on the other hand, acts as a provider and also lacks the locally elected base to underpin, say, the hearing of complaints – hence its score of 3.

- The funding council is shown as discounting the need for skills for employment to a slightly greater extent than the purchasing model. Why? Our rating is based on the tendency of funding councils to minimise direct intervention – but we remain uncertain of our scoring here. Beyond this issue we see a risk that all single purpose educational entities will strain against direct vocational training for employment, following the traditional pattern of professional responses to vocational education and the historical place of academic work over vocational work in the education hierarchy.

- The funding council and single purpose purchaser are both shown as emphasising monitoring of specified standards more strongly than the multi purpose purchaser. Again, why? This is based on the requirement to balance education with other services in the multi purpose model, which is likely to generate cross service monitoring which may in turn dilute educational monitoring. The judgement is a fine one and we might equally have indicated a scoring of 5 in the multi purpose model.

- In relation to monitoring specified standards, the White Paper application is shown as offering only a medium commitment, despite government emphasis on Standard Assessment Tasks (SATs), exam results and the like. This is because the commitment extends only to measuring tested outputs whilst the emphasis on assessing need in the purchasing model implies a commitment to monitoring against needs as well as outputs

- Similarly, is the single purpose purchaser more likely to emphasise the need for convergent priorities with other public services than a funding council? We think so because of the possibility that the single purpose purchaser will be elected and so reflect the democratic base of adjacent services; but we accept this point to be tenuous.

- Does the White Paper really discount convergence with other services to the extent shown (a score of 2)? We believe so, because whilst it allows some convergence with other services in areas where opting out is not extensive, its active provisions push towards a single purpose funding agency and GM schools, isolated from other services. It also envisages further central government intervention in setting education budgets through, for example, national formulae.

- Why should the professional-electoral model emphasise the community need for democratic representation more strongly than its post-1945 counterpart? Because an elected framework coupled with the separation of provision from purchasing allows for more vigorous representation.

- Why would any model discount the importance of compliance with statute? Our scoring is not intended to imply that it would – rather it attempts to reflect the extent to which models promote needs beyond compliance with statute.

- Does not the provision for education associations in the White Paper emphasise the need for the improvement of performance more strongly than the post-1945 application? We think not. Whilst there are new powers for LEAs and for the Secretary of State to intervene, these are in reality limited to replacing governing bodies and by implication, staff. There is evidence, from past good practice, that correcting poor performance entails sustained professional support and intervention which is largely precluded under the combined provisions of the Schools Act 1992 and the White Paper.

- Why is the individualistic model shown as 3 and the White Paper as 2 in relation to professional discretion – surely both models allow maximum discretion of schools? It is because the discretion allowed in the White Paper is managerial rather than professional. The individualistic model allows professional discretion only as far as market choices coincide with professional judgement.

- There are wide variations shown between the models in their treatment of the need for a public account of their affairs. Why? On the face of it, all publicly funded entities have to give a public account of their affairs. The difference we attempt to capture is between those models which attend to this need on the basis of values and those which attend to it as a side issue and because of statutory compulsion. So the multi purpose purchaser from its emphasis on the value of social cohesion and democracy will emphasise this more than its single purpose counterpart. The individualistic model will give less emphasis because there is less decision making or public action for which account must be made. The White Paper, whilst prescriptive about the account which LEAs must make, is less clear on grant maintained schools and takes a fairly narrow range of issues on which reports must be made.

- All models require resource allocation at some level. The variation between the models relates mostly to the extent to which the need for resource allocation is related to a need for influence and control. Although the purchasing models tend more to non intervention and hence a discounting of this need, they do also specify cost and therefore maintain an emphasis on this need. Again, we invite readers to apply our method of distinguishing between the models in order to reach their own conclusions.

OVERALL EMPHASES DISCERNABLE ACROSS THE MODELS

The elected democratic and purchasing models and the post-1945 applications are shown as allowing more needs and emphasising these more heavily than others. This is not to propose that the models are driven by the assessment of needs – only that they emphasise their role in making good deficits and in interpreting and meeting needs. The individual school boards also emphasise needs, particularly pupils needs, but here the capacity is constrained by size. The capacity to emphasise community needs in particular is constrained, because individual school communities can only rarely be related to discrete community boundaries; more often individual school boards will compete across overlapping, indistinct boundaries. Furthermore, individual schools are inevitably more strongly driven by existing parent and pupil needs.

The individualistic model appears to be singled out in discounting needs. Is this really the case? In so far as this model deliberately moves away from a needs and dependency culture, it is likely because the emphasis is on choice rather than need. Concern for posterity appears more clearly in the community agency models.

The distinction between the single purpose purchaser and funding council model is hard to hold in terms of needs. The two models are indeed similar, the main distinctions being the reporting of one directly to a local community and of the other to central government and the purchasing emphasis on needs assessment and restraint from provision. Under the current applications of this model the tendency of funding councils has been towards non intervention and to discouraging dependency. Hence our score, but it is true that this might change in future. Our decision to score on the basis of current patterns is based on our use of models which might conceivably be implemented within the next decade.

CONCLUSION

Our project assumed that understanding educational needs is central to understanding and improving the ways in which needs are met. It also assumed that different value systems would recognise and explore different needs and that emphasis on different needs would in turn lead to different functions. Some of these differences in responding to needs are clear cut and derive obviously from the value frame for each model. Other differences are less sharply defined, not least because needs and functions also overlap. For example, the community has a need for its wants and needs to be assessed; if this need is to be met, some entity must establish a function to meet that need – but, some models will do this through political and professional judgement and others will do it through holistic analysis and others through the operation of choice. The comparison of the models therefore demands that a functional critique should follow a study of needs.

CHAPTER 7

Functions

We have said that functions are statements of activities which an entity will feel responsible for performing. In the UK, LEAs have depended largely on governing legislation for power to perform their functions albeit within the persisting severity of the *ultra vires* rule. Legislation thus provides a principal frame for functions. But even in the most law bound systems, many functions derive from the entity's own agenda for action. For example, some local authorities in the 1980s created policies of economic development and others declared themselves nuclear free zones, neither of them explicitly mandated powers.

We will be analysing functions that must be fulfilled if needs are to be met, so that our models of governance can be assessed in terms of their capacity to ensure that functions are fulfilled adequately.

There are several ways in which functions can be inferred. For example, the Audit Commission (1989) in commenting on the post-1988 functions described LEAs as 'Losing an Empire and Finding a Role' which would include elements of six distinct approaches. The LEA will be:

1 A leader/visionary, setting overall policy objectives and defining the context within which institutions will operate.

2 A partner, giving support, help and guidance, as they achieve autonomy.

3 A planner, involving a more sensitive and consensual basis for facilities planning, and based on an objective assessment of need.

4 An information provider, particularly concerned to enhance the exercise of choice.

5 A regulator/buyer, in which the authority is envisaged as entering into contracts with suppliers of education.

6 a bank manager, which will involve reaching decisions on levels of resources, and linking them to planning.

It commented that 'although LEAs may have lost their empires there remains an important role for them to play. Schools and colleges can benefit from support and leadership... there is also a vital role in monitoring and assuring quality and providing information to parents, students, and governors to allow them to carry out their new responsibilities.'

These somewhat general and optimistic accounts of LEA functions can be matched by other more prosaic statements of perceived functions of LEAs implied by the 1988 Act, and from the current legislation. The first line functions which LEAs must fulfil would thus comprise:

- provision of educational institutions
- ensuring that all institutions provided education to those within the compulsory school ages and that the curriculum for the school satisfied the legal requirements to provide the National Curriculum
- ensuring that children attended school
- ensuring that pupils were tested at the ages of 7, 11, 14 and 16
- voting resources for education
- making statements for pupils with special needs
- providing assessment, education and associated facilities
- providing careers service.

Such functions might also be expressed within the traditional, rationalistic model of functions which so many local authorities, following the Maud and Bains Reports in the late 1960s, and with the then earnest encouragement of government, sought to implement, as shown in Figure 7.1.

ALLOWING LINKAGE BETWEEN FUNCTIONS

If we then turn to chart functions in ways which are closely related to the enumeration of needs contained in Chapter 6, we would also state the linkages between them (Figure 7.2). In this we distinguish between first line, second line and development functions. First line functions result in outcomes by way of services or goods that directly relate to the achievement of policies. It is, however, a commonplace of organisational life that first line functions need the support of second line functions to ensure their achievement. Thus staffing the schools is not an objective in itself but an essential prerequisite of providing teaching and learning. Devel-

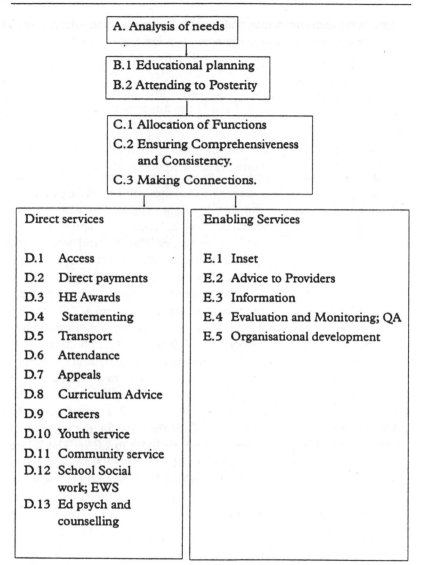

Figure 7.1 A rational operational planning model of functions

opment functions support the identification and specification of future first line functions.

Immediately, we can see that the allocation of first line functions is contestable territory. Is it the DFE, or LEAs, or governors or funding councils which now provide institutions? Is future planning – determining the future shape of an area's education – a legitimate aim for a public authority, or one that results incrementally and intuitively from the hidden hand of the market driven by consumer wants? Or, conversely, is it possible to imagine a public authority which is not concerned with helping to predict the needs and shape the future of its service?

These questions arise both in the future and as we look back at the holistic and all powerful LEA prescribed in 1944 and the greatly limited LEA of the 1988 Act.

First line functions generate a large number of second line functions, such as regulating the appointment of teachers and providing for their professional development; creating building programmes and building schools; making financial estimates; creating formulae and providing and controlling finance and generating resources. The first and second line functions encompassed by previous British local education systems are displayed in Figure 7.2. They leave very little out and they display a sequence and enumeration of functions not far different from that of the post-1944 LEA operating a rationalistic planning system at full stretch.

But functions are determined ultimately as a matter of political choice. The 1992 White Paper allows only a minimal set of functions to LEAs (See p.42–43), allowing, for example, the right to 'only trade at the margin of capacity', in the expectation that private concerns will take on the trading functions that some LEAs have developed since 1988. Yet the White Paper, and other models which combine both a consumer driven and a centralist policy, do not dispose of the case for the exercise of functions even when they cease to attribute them to LEAs. The White Paper itself re-introduces functions omitted from ERA. Also funding councils and the DFE are gradually making functions explicit, as those which may have been overlooked are re-introduced incrementally and often in new forms. The importance of such a list is to explain what can or should or should not be abandoned, whatever the model of governance preferred. On that basis, we have made an analytic grouping of the functions in Figure 7.1. This is reduced to place blocks of the same functions in organisational relationship with each other (Figure 7.2).

We urge the reader to use the diagram in a way different from that of the 1960s planners, and to ask whether an education system, whether operating through the hidden hand of the market or through centralist planning, can dispose of any of these functions, either as a guide to future action or as a check on what has been provided. This need not preempt the question of whether there is authority in a system to hold together the

A – FIRST LINE FUNCTIONS

(a) Providing Institutions	(b) Providing Education	(c) Providing Resources	(d) Meeting Special Needs	(e) Providing Associated With Education (e.g. Careers)	(f) Future

B – SECOND LINE FUNCTIONS

(a) Staffing	(d) Operational Monitoring & Evaluation
(b) Buildings	(e) Reviewing Provision
(c) Finance	(f) Reorganisation of Services

C – DEVELOPMENT FUNCTIONS

(a) Operational Planning – needs analysis
(b) Educational Planning
(c) Policy Evaluation and Monitoring
(d) Organisation Development

Figure 7.2 – The range of LEA functions constructed from 1988 Act

performance of these functions in some holistic unity. The analysis in Figure 7.2 also helps us examine the 1992 White Paper to see what is to be left of the post-1945 system.

What functions would appear in the 1992 models? What is disposed of, not simply from the work of the residual LEA, or the greatly strengthened governing body or the new funding council, but from the system altogether? We conclude not very much. The issue is not what will have to be done, but which entity will do it, within which style of governing mechanism.

The White Paper of 1992 does not in fact specify in detail the functions of the funding agency or governing bodies. Will they in any sense make a needs assessment and attempt to relate GM places to those in LEA maintained schools? Will they attempt to predict future provision in the light of demography and economic trends? How will specialisations in the curriculum be distributed between 'outlets'?

The range of functions is one issue. It is likely that some important options will disappear in the consumer driven and funding council models although these may eventually re-emerge. For example in these models there will be a reduction in democratic input and the work that goes with it. There will be perhaps less concern with minority groups of pupils, although that is not a necessary consequence of the governing arrangements in themselves, merely a likely outcome of pursuing numerically driven and remote policies. There will be less attention to the community functions of education.

The second issue is connection between sets of functions. Evaluation and monitoring, for example, have several potential outcomes. They enable quality to be assessed and assured. But the same knowledge which is generated can feed back into curriculum development and into its modes of delivery. Evaluation and monitoring are also a knowledge base in a reiterative cycle of making judgements about what is provided (evaluation), what should be provided (needs) and how to provide it (planning). If these functions are distributed among different entities it is likely to make the exploitation of knowledge and judgements the weaker.

SUMMATIVE COMPARISONS

In our field work, discussion of needs which must be met for individuals, communities and providers produced many answers which were, in effect, statements of functions which remained whether essential or highly desirable. These statements were what individual professionals, users or politicians thought to be appropriate, and were of course value based and therefore contestable.

In Table 7.1 we present the functions emerging from fieldwork and analysis in abbreviated but connected form. The connections and summary we present are based on the various analyses outlined in this chapter and on the rational operational planning model.

The rational model inevitably implies assumptions about educational systems, namely that an overriding entity starts logically, if not chronologically, by assessing needs, before planning and allocating provision, and that the resulting services are then evaluated with a view to ensuring a reiterative cycle of action again starting with an assessment of needs. It is recognised that the sequence asserted may be disputed but its elements appear in all models and some consistent frame is needed to reveal what is lost and what is gained. The organisation of functions from our fieldwork into this framework is therefore used as the basis for testing each of our models and the historical and White Paper applications are tested.

Table 7.1 Functions emphasised in the models of governance

| | CONCEPTUAL MODELS | | | | | | | HISTORICAL APPLICATIONS | |
| | COMMUNITY AGENCY | | | GOVERNMENT AGENCY | | | | Post-1945 | White Paper |
Functions models	Professional /electoral	Single Purpose	Multi-Purpose	Individual School Board (CA)	Individual School Board (GA)	Funding Council	Individualistic		
Needs analysis	3	4	4	3	3	3	1	3	1
Planning	5	3	4	2	3	3	1	4	2
Shaping implementation strategies	5	3	3	1	3	4	1	5	2
Organising links	5	1	4	2	1	1	1	5	1
Resource allocation	5	3	3	1	3	3	3	5	3
Teaching and learning	5	5	5	5	5	5	5	5	5
Associated educational services	5	2	3	1	1	3	2	5	2
Associated organisational services	5	1	2	1	1	1	1	5	1
Monitoring and evaluation	3	3	3	3	3	3	5	2	5
Advice, quality assurance	5	2	3	1	3	2	3	5	2
Information	5	3	3	1	3	3	2	2	2
Providing INSET	5	2	2	1	3	2	1	5	2
Political representation	5	1	4	3	1	1	1	5	1
Social reporting	3	2	3	2	1	1	3	3	1
Adjudication	5	4	4	2	3	3	3	5	3

Table 7.2 Planning

Functions models	Professional /electoral	Single Purpose	Multi-Purpose	Individual School Board (CA)	Individual School Board (GA)	Funding Council	Individualistic	Post-1945	White Paper
Planning	5	3	4	2	3	3	1	4	2

A COMPARISON OF SPECIFIC FUNCTIONS

As with values and needs, we shall start our analysis by taking examples of functions and working systematically across all the models.

The professional-electoral model would give strong emphasis to planning, because the blending of democratic and professional perspectives requires it. Articulating views of electorates with functions requires planning and emphasising professional direction in public services: there is some structuring of priorities in time sequence in order to secure improvement.

The purchasing models also emphasise the planning of purchasing but isolate this from the planning of provision; the multi-purpose purchaser will emphasise planning further in order to facilitate prioritisation and coordination across a range of public services.

Planning for individual school boards would be limited to organisational development since they would be single entities. Of course, organisational development requires some thought about intra-institutional relationships, and in strongly market driven versions of individual school boards, there is likely to be a good deal of attention on marketing research and external relations which brings a particular kind of planning into play. It is also possible that a government agency version of this model might emphasise planning given the greater planning capacity of a government level system.

A funding council would be likely to emphasise planning to a moderate degree, in order to maintain an overview and holistic sense of direction. But, again, the commitment to limited intervention and maximised delegation would place firm boundaries on such a function.

The individualistic model would discount formal, regulatory planning, substituting the aggregation of choices for this function, although providers would be drawn towards marketing planning techniques based on, for example, marketing and market research.

In the decades since 1945, local authorities emphasised planning structures, although the short term span of council remits, and the focus on constituency business (particularly for those with annual, one third elections) constrained an otherwise central function.

Finally, the White Paper proposes new powers regarding school building and closure, thus reinstating some powers removed by ERA. However, the strength of the moves towards opting out and of DFE statements that the funding agency would not be a planning authority contradict these steps and produce a relatively weak emphasis overall.

All models require a measure of emphasis on resource allocation, but the extent to which a model emphasises resource allocation as a direct means of meeting a need, realising a value or pursuing a specific policy varies significantly.

Table 7.3 Resource allocation

Functions models	*Professional /electoral*	*Single Purpose*	*Multi-Purpose*	*Individual School Board (CA)*	*Individual School Board (GA)*	*Funding Council*	*Individualistic Post-1945*	*White Paper*
Resource allocation	5	3	3	1	3	3	3	5	3

So, the professional electoral model is likely to use resource allocation to reinforce professional and democratic values and to secure influence.

Both purchasing models and the funding council models will use resourcing to secure influence, but will be more constrained. In each case, allocation of resources for provision will only serve to influence at the point at which contracts are made.

In the individual school board models, some variation might also be discerned. A community agency almost inevitably implies a national funding formula, since the board replaces local government whilst emphasising direct local accountability for the school. For a board which is a central government agent, there is scope for a wider range of models which allows the government agency to choose the extent to which tailored, targeted allocations are used as carrots and sticks as alternatives to simple national formulae.

SPECIFIC EXAMPLES OF VARIATIONS BETWEEN SUB SETS

As can be seen, not all models are distinctive in any one respect. Significant alignments or variations may occur between different models at different points so that, for example, functions for the purchasing models will be similar except, say, in relation to political representation, planning and organising links.

Both individual school board models have similar approaches to functions with regard to needs analysis, delivery of teaching and learning, delivery of educational and organisational services, quality assurance and the provision of advice. But they differ, for example, whenever central government capacity allows for a more extensive function, for example, on determining strategies, information or planning.

Table 7.4 School boards compared														
Models/functions	Needs analysis	Planning	Shaping implementation strategies	Organising links	Resource allocation	Teaching and learning	Associated educational services	Associated organisational services	Monitoring and evaluation	Advice, quality assurance	Information	Providing INSET	Political represenetation	Social reporting	Adjudication
School Board (CA)	3	2	1	2	1	5	1	1	3	1	1	1	3	2	2
School Board (GA)	3	3	3	1	3	5	1	1	3	3	3	3	1	1	3

There are even greater similarities between the single purpose purchaser and funding council models in relation to functions. However, the means of carrying out a function may differ more strongly so that, for example, the funding council has the option of delivering associated educational or organisational services which would not be available to the single purpose purchaser.

The professional electoral model and the historical application are also self evidently similar in many respects. However, we have shown a much stronger emphasis on needs analysis, monitoring and evaluation, quality assurance and advice in the conceptual, professional-electoral model than in its historical counterpart to reflect the possibility of overcoming past weaknesses.

The individualistic model stands out as being the most distinctive. It discounts strongly more functions than any other, achieving a score of one in eight cases, largely because it is anticipated that facilitating individual choice will supersede a large range of functions.

Models/functions	Needs analysis	Planning	Shaping implementation strategies	Organising links	Resource allocation	Teaching and learning	Associated educational services	Associated organisational services	Monitoring and evaluation	Advice, quality assurance	Information	Providing INSET	Political represenetation	Social reporting	Adjudication
Table 7.5 The SPP and FC models															
Single purpose purchaser (SPP)	4	3	3	1	3	5	2	1	3	2	3	2	1	2	4
Funding Council (FC)	3	3	4	1	3	5	3	1	3	2	3	2	1	1	3

Uncertainties

The individualistic model does not itself allow for needs analysis; instead it allows for the expression of wants through individual choice. It is for this reason that a score of 1 has been allocated, but this does not in any way imply that this is a provider driven system – far from it.

All models will call for individual entities to shape their own strategies. What is assessed here is the extent to which determining strategies at the level of the system is allowed. Thus, the community agency individual school board, like the individualistic model, scores 1, simply because the level of intervention between school and a non interventionist central government is low.

The associated educational services are taken as including specialist curriculum support such as technology buses, specialist centres or peripatetic music teaching. Although it is unlikely that a funding council would provide such services, unlike the purchasing models, it could if it so wished; hence the score of 3.

Advice and quality assurance are intended to encompass what was referred to in our fieldwork as 'Making it better'. In fact only the professional-electoral and post-1945 models emphasise this intrinsically.

The purchaser models might ensure that such advice were available as part of regulating the market but would certainly not provide it directly. The community agency individual school board provides no vehicle to allow emphasis on this since the only entities are the school, from where the problem arises, and central government, which would be too remote to provide a hands on service.

It is already recognised in many post-ERA authorities, and it was clear in our fieldwork, that information about the system as a whole, whether informal or formal, quantitative or qualitative, is seen as increasingly important by those managing educational entities. However, it is costly to collect and aggregate and it is also seen as an instrument of power. Therefore non interventionist models discount this function, and interventionist and non interventionist models have to balance a desire for information against cost. There is a paradox for the more atomistic models also. The greater the fragmentation in the system, the more intense the need for overview information – and the harder it is to collect.

As with values and needs, there are apparent contradictions and ambiguities. For example:

- Although the individualistic model might discount controlling the delivery of educational or organisational services, it will not necessarily discount delivery by a third party.
- Did the post-1945 pattern really discount monitoring and evaluation to the extent that a score of 2 is justified? What about the work of inspectors? The low score reflects the much less public structured and explicit approach to monitoring and evaluation pursued previously, but it is recognised that the implicit professional judgements of inspectors were indeed evaluative. It is also recognised that although the White Paper adopts the provisions of the Schools Act 1992 and so emphasises evaluation, it weakens the system's monitoring capacity. Nonetheless, the inspection provisions are so clear and represent such an absolute commitment to evaluation through inspection that a score of 5 has been allocated.
- All except the professional-electoral and 1945 models are shown as discounting an advisory function; is this too extreme? In fact some advice might flow from the need for educational leadership stated in Chapter 5. Our inference is that this would be more likely to take the form of INSET, delivery of associated educational services (like specialist language or IT support) or the output of monitoring and evaluation.

- The emphasis on social reporting in the individualistic model may seem surprising. It is based upon our judgement that there would need to be some accountability and communication between the school and central government, if for no other reason than to diffuse complaints to MPs and questions in the House.

OVERALL PATTERNS BETWEEN MODELS

As the analysis reaches the operational end of the governance process, choices become firmer and consequences clearer. The readings from Table 7.1 also confirm what one would expect from this analysis. Thus, organisational linkages are more likely to be sponsored by a multi than by a single purpose purchaser, and more strongly sponsored in the professional-electoral model and its historical manifestation. The individualistic model, followed by individual school board models, are restrained from interventionist functions. No model does other than strongly allow for teaching and learning (although each may adopt very different delivery mechanisms). Quality assurance would be implicit rather than explicit in the professional-electoral model but it would be present in all models, reflecting an increased understanding of previous shortcomings in this domain.

Table 7.6 The PE and Post-1945 models

Models/functions	Needs analysis	Planning	Shaping implementation strategies	Organising links	Resource allocation	Teaching and learning	Associated educational services	Associated organisational services	Monitoring and evaluation	Advice, quality assurance	Information	Providing INSET	Political represenetation	Social reporting	Adjudication
Professional-electoral	3	5	5	5	5	5	5	5	3	5	5	5	5	3	5
Post 1945	3	4	5	5	5	5	5	5	2	4	2	5	5	3	5

However, this set of perceptions can and should be tested by a parallel holistic analysis; styles of functioning will certainly differ between models, and the nature of such variations is explained in our next chapter, but relative emphasis between functions may vary more than emphasis between values and needs; so we urge the reader to complete the analysis for themselves.

CHAPTER 8

Modes of Operation

We can now move on from the analytic frames in previous chapters to assess the benefits and difficulties that might be associated with different models of governance.

The different models incorporate different value preferences. Of their nature, value preferences themselves are not susceptible to testing, but their consequences in terms of the needs met and the functions fulfilled can be. Chapters 5–7 have shown what packages of values, needs and functions are to be found in each model. In this Chapter we examine some of their consequences in terms of how well they might perform their ascribed purposes.

In doing so we raise the following questions:

- What will each model deliver?
- What will be the cost of moving to and maintaining each model?
- What kind of structure and mechanisms will each model require?
- Going beyond costs and structures, what are the expressive and psychological aspects of each model?

Starting with these questions we can list the criteria against which to assess the models as shown in Figure 8.1, the application of which will be discussed in the following paragraphs.

WHAT WILL THE MODEL DELIVER?

The most important elements of what each model aims to deliver are analysed in Chapters 5–7: the values emphasised, the needs to be met and the functions to be performed. These can be regarded as intended outcomes of different arrangements. The capacity of each model, however, to produce its expected outcomes will be affected by the nature and amount of the inputs, and of the processes which it entails. In these terms it is possible to depict each of the models as follows:

Principal criteria

1. Values endorsed
2. Needs met
3 Functions performed

What each model delivers

1.. Inputs to and outputs from each model
2. Nature of process

Costs

1. Costs to systems and intermediate entity including
   1.1 Dismantling existing structures (redundancies, etc)
   1.2 Consultants
   1.3 New central agencies
   1.4 LEA administration and advice
   1.5 Servicing LEA committees system to seeking direction from councillors
   1.6 Servicing corporate working
2. Costs to school/institutions
   2.1 Reduced scale of purchasing goods
   2.2 Distraction
   2.3 Use of private consultants for expert services
   2.4 Learning new roles
   2.5 Transfer costs of administration
   2.6 Running governing bodies
3. Costs to clients
   3.1 Finding their way to new providers

Mechanics and structures

1. Size of system: span of control versus viability (e.g. central contact as 25,000 institutions)
2.. Size of systems for competent information flows
3. Limitations and advantages of purchaser-provider mechanisms
   3.1 Maturity of providers and purchasers
   3.2 Time and content specified contracts; continuity of providers' services; over specification
4. Modes of democracy
   4.1 Remote versus proximate democracy
   4.2 Degree of legitimation
5. Role of professions
   5.1 Degree of client power and market power
   5.2 Capacity of new systems professionalism
   5.3 Capacity of new educational professionalism
6. Connections between services
7. Feasibility of centre carrying enlarged role

Figure 8.1 List of criteria by which to assess each model of governance

Expressive and psychological
1. Power generated at different levels
2. Commitment generated within entities
3. Location and quality of leadership
4. Development of new professionalism

Figure 8.1 List of criteria by which to assess each model of governance

The PE model assumes the maximum possible input because of an assumption that its purpose is to make good deficiencies. It also assumes there will be the maximum of both political input and professional care extended on the performance of the functions.

The processes will be maximal, because the model assumes that providers will work within a rational planning model which allows for maximum input from both political leaders and professional advisers. It is also associated with considerable freedom for the schools in such matters as the curriculum and in making their own relationships with the community and clients.

The outcomes are also likely to be maximal, in that the model is directed to a comprehensive and holistic range of values, needs and functions.

But the inputs might be excessive, inviting too much activity and inefficient empire building.

The SPP and MPP models assume a maximum input in that they, too, espouse both rationalistic planning and allow for democratic control.

They expect, however, somewhat more parsimonious processes because the intermediate entity will purchase rather than provide services, other than those required for the purchasing activity itself. In doing so, purchasers will prescribe the quality, quantity and cost of services but will not be involved in the mechanism of provision.

The processes of provision will, in fact, involve the providers – mainly schools – in many of the processes hitherto undertaken by local authorities.

Both individual school board models assume rather less input because of the absence of an intermediary agency and because the schools and central government will be unable to undertake local interpretation on any significant scale.

The key distinguishing feature within the community agency models is that of the purchaser – provider division, within a mechanism capable of serving a wide range of value preferences. All of these assume a powerful intermediary entity committed to strong consultation and to performing a wide range of functions. Its promise is to deliver services more efficiently and with stronger deference to client demands and needs than would the PE model.

The government agency models, including the funding council and individualistic by contrast, allow for an abbreviated, even minimalist, approach to inputs and processes, in that they avoid the electoral contribution and needs based processes. All but the funding council eschew rational planning. But they expect clear outcomes in terms of strongly framed educational content and performance delivered under the sanctions of combined central control and consumer choice.

COSTS: THE COST OF MOVING TO AND MAINTAINING EACH MODEL

We comment now, as far as we can, on the differences in cost of installing and maintaining each model. There is no systematic evidence of costs likely to result from the White Paper arrangements, or against which we can test the models, either of restructuring the whole system or of maintaining the patterns that might emerge. This is surprising in a government committed to the reduction and control of public expenditure. There is no public information on the increased costs falling to the DFE in supporting GM schools, or in creating quangos such as the funding agency. The White Paper – Education Bill system promotes choices which are likely to generate surplus places to be maintained yet promises tighter control of surplus places. Functions will remain to be performed by new and immature entities that will have to learn to re-invent wheels, all with the help of private agencies. For a while at least, there will be duplication between LEAs and the new entities. At the same time, we do not know how much waste and ineffective capacity is locked up in LEA or central government administration, and what savings will ensue from dismantling old systems or achieving economies of scale in supporting GM schools.

In the PE model, where services are provided by the entity beyond the school, economy of scale achieved through bulk purchase, and expert input into purchasing, have been seen as advantages although they are not intrinsic to the model; they could run equally well on either direct management or local management of schools. In any case, the economic case is giving way under technical changes in purchasing systems. In those models, such as the individualistic or public purchaser models, which allow maximum freedom to purchase, units as large as some secondary schools are likely to secure good discounts by themselves and 'just in time' stock keeping reduces the pressure for bulk purchase. There will be some flexibility gained by schools in not having to use an intermediate stage.

The use of an entity beyond the school for purchasing is justified by the need to purchase specialist equipment, particularly in IT, and perhaps to certain items of scientific, domestic science and PE equipment, where expertise in specification and purchasing may not always be available to a school. Establishing consortia among schools for these purposes would carry time and other costs, but in some areas of our field work, a private entity had successfully facilitated this. In other areas the LEA has established its teams as trading units. Although some schools on LMS might prefer to go elsewhere, others, (and some FE colleges) have preferred to buy in to the LEA arrangements.

An argument against the PE model has been its tendency to maximise services and intervention; its traditional manifestations have certainly created additional activities and found it difficult to revoke or reduce functions once established. Recent changes have demonstrated that there is scope for increased efficiency. But without long term research on results and costings the benefits can not be weighed and neither can the opportunity costs.

Another concern is the cost of the democratic process, particularly when it is coupled with a professional process which might move in an opposite direction. Achieving accommodation between the two perspectives is costly and time consuming. In our field work, appreciation of these checks and balances was usually tempered by a desire for professional and managerial efficiency in all issues except those of grand strategy: the PE model was seen as an important safety net and provider of leadership but by some as an impediment in processes of management and administration.

DISTRACTION

In our field work, many said that the disadvantage of working without a providing intermediary body was that heads would be required to undertake administrative and other tasks that might well prove to be a distraction from their main duties as educational and school leaders. Buying in services hitherto provided by an LEA would be a costly business and it would take time to specify needs in such a way as to be able to identify and then commission providers of goods and services of the right quality and price. Even if heads formed consortia for these purposes one of them would have to undertake the work previously undertaken by a local authority, or they would have to employ a purchasing officer. Similar points were raised about commissioning private school transport. In the small sample of heads consulted these disadvantages outweighed the advantages of being free to go to whichever seller one wanted. There is evidence that GM schools are trying to counteract these difficulties by looking for long term suppliers, thus losing the benefit of the freedom to tender.

EXPERT SERVICES

A further set of problems concerns provision of certain expert or professional services. Educational psychology and counselling are thought difficult to provide by private consultancies. The need for these services is 'lumpy' and not presented in an even flow. A school would thus find it difficult to contend with a large number of unexpected difficult cases at once. Yet Coventry, the LEA with the least developed arguments for selling services in most other respects, has delegated budgets for psychological services and the psychologists and the schools both reported useful outcomes involving schools closely in prioritisation, providing that an intermediary safety net was available. Their arguments against 'privatising' educational psychology were more to do with processes than evening out 'lumpy' needs. Educational psychologists need continuity of contact with pupils, families and schools so as to sustain knowledge of family background and school milieu. This would be difficult if undertaken on a consultancy basis. They also need an understanding of the full range of educational provision in an area to develop properly informed statements of needs. Sudden changes in patterns of referrals can be important indicators of changing educational needs and school performance data which should be fed into holistic needs assessment.

Whilst a minority of interviewees thought it possible to provide legal services *ad hoc*, most believed that expertise in educational matters was more competently accumulated in a local authority service than by individual firms of solicitors. Many cases needed careful working through in terms of precedent, and a time limited private service was unlikely to devote that time to it. The costs of wrong or incomplete advice were seen as unacceptable and the likelihood of such advice as being greater in an atomised service.

There is less certainty about the usefulness and expertise that schools derive from advisory services. Many secondary schools have a professional educational staff larger than that of the LEA service. They might be able to secure help which they identify as necessary from the many educational institutions involved in educational studies. However, school expertise was primarily in day to day delivery for the curriculum. Some external source of advice which can promote improvement and innovation is seen as necessary. Furthermore, without some entity beyond the school small and isolated schools, and schools that needed help but were unlikely to seek it, ought to have available a continuing source of guided support.

A further point concerns the insurance defence function. There are 'lumpy', one-off expenditures which can only be covered over a long time span, and which could cripple a single school budget. A fire can be covered by commercially purchased insurance but the other elements of cover, for example, designing and commissioning a replacement building and finding temporary accommodation, are likely to be beyond the capacity of a single school. So might be heavy legal cost or the work involved in employment issues with appearances at tribunals and the like.

USING PRIVATE CONSULTANTS

In moving from the use of full scale entities beyond the school to free standing institutions, it is assumed in some models that schools will be able to secure the expert services they need from privately commissioned consultants. There are clear advantages in doing so: they need be paid for only the work they do; there are no costs in employing or dismissing incompetent professionals; they are not be tied to LEA practices and policies; and operating in the competitive market rather than on an assured pay-roll makes consultants mean and keen.

There are disadvantages, too, which are more obvious in those areas of activity likely to require long-term commitment to the servicing of clients. Many school related problems require knowledge of the milieu, and of the environment and problems of individual clients. All consultants require time to make inroads into a problem and its context and there are costs in discontinuity. All but the largest consultancies are likely to lack the full range of expertise and have to sub-contract it. Consultants themselves commonly suffer from having no back-up structure which can research the market for their services, ensure they are involved in follow-up, and provide them with time for exploration and self-development. Where such support does exist it is reflected in costs. Again, there is no public information about the costs of or value for money given by consultancy projects; they are assumed to be indisputedly better than services provided by a public service entity which are not trusted by some to delegate its powers.

There is evidence that all small, and many large, companies fail to invest in sufficient research and development. This is seen as the cause of the low skills cycle in the British economy. Unless an intermediary body or central government identifies R & D needs and purchases it, the capacity to carry it out, as well as its direct output, might disappear. A particularly worrying example of this trend emerges in INSET, where devolution to schools has led to significant reductions in work in advancing the skills of specialist teachers. Instead, resources are channelled into main stream delivery. Where will future advisory teachers, inspectors and consultants come from?

THE COSTS OF IMPLEMENTING PRESENT PROPOSALS

Government has caused there to be several 'reforms' of structure in the NHS and in local government. All of these generate costs in redundancies, the setting up and recruitment for wholly new structures, and the cost of orientating newcomers to work in unfamiliar settings. Causing teams to work together and to know their remit well is also a heavy cost which is wasted whenever existing structures are broken up. In the case of the 1988 reforms there were heavy costs in breaking up old systems and in installing the new local management systems. The fees to accountants alone must have been great. These costs may be proper and lead to improvement, but without public account they can not be evaluated.

The proposals of the White Paper will be costly to implement. For some while, whilst the LEAs linger on with increasingly reduced functions, there will be dual control and imposed collaboration between LEAs and the funding agency. Other costs will arise from the operation of the Office for Standards in Education, education associations, and the National Curriculum Council.

FUND RAISING

A large issue which did not emerge fully in our project was whether, as a consequence of the shift to the centre, education should be funded through a specified 100% grant by the national authority. If this is the case, the need for and role of elected members in raising local taxes would be removed and the need for prioritisation between other competing local public services would be reduced. In such circumstances there would be fewer objections to the single purpose models which might well be more efficient. But as far as our fieldwork and consultations were concerned, there was a widespread conviction that a central government would be reluctant to gather to itself all the criticism presently absorbed locally – particularly as the inevitable raft of winners and losers which would sail into view with a national funding formula for all educational services would make seductive press copy. Respondents and critics for our study felt that whilst the possibility would be explored and whilst a national formula for schools might emerge, some local safety valve would still be needed.

THE MECHANISMS AND STRUCTURES THAT EACH MODEL WILL REQUIRE

There are several organisational criteria by which the different models can be judged.

Appropriate size of systems

Two of the models invite anxiety about their capacity to ensure competent control over and contact with over 20,000 schools which they will fund and monitor. A napoleonic model is proposed so far only in respect of the curriculum. It seems likely that eventually it would have to administer its controls through a system of regional offices. It would differ from the PE and MPP models in being free of local democratic controls and from both of those models and the SPP in being somewhat more parsimonious in the range of values, needs and functions with which it was concerned. The individual school board model, whilst emphasising the single institution, ironically creates a superstructure with a span of control which is unlikely to be capable of meeting school needs.

On grounds of span and control, therefore, some intermediate entity seems unavoidable, and this is the common feature of the public agency models. Indeed, in many existing LEAs divisional structures have proved necessary in order to offset centralisation of individual and day-to-day administration.

An aspect of size of system concerns the flow of information. The public agency models allow for the circulation of information between clients, providers and the resource and planning authorities. The government agency models assume greater degrees of autonomy and therefore of isolation from the larger system. In these models, it is not clear that individualistic providers are expected to tap into larger information and knowledge systems. Neither the DFE nor a funding agency is expected to be near enough its institutions. There will thus be no opportunity for the 'hot' knowledge, developed by practitioners in contact with clients, (Martin Rein, 1983) to be converted into the 'cold' knowledge that should be the starting point for policy and practice.

The nature of markets

The MPP, SPP, FC and individualistic models imply some form of purchaser-provider arrangements. Such arrangements overlap with and have been confused with market arrangements. But they are not identical. In a free market, each individual is expected to optimise his or her own advantage. The aggregate of individual decisions to buy and sell will create adequate services and goods through the mechanism of supply and demand, and will also ensure that new goods and services are developed by providers.

The education service cannot meet many of the conditions of the free market. The purchasers do not have money at their disposal to use as they wish among the full range of goods and services. The providers are not working to improve their own pecuniary position. The services being offered contain esoteric elements, and information about them is not likely to be available to many of the clients so that choice will somewhat constrained. Many of the services are offered without much direct client voice as to their nature: for example, the national curriculum is prescribed centrally and is a product akin to that provided by an old fashioned nationalised industry rather than by a free market.

The more accurate description would therefore be that of a purchaser provider system. It is clear that such a system can operate in a range of models embracing different values. It is feasible within the PE, MPP and SPP models as well as in the individual school board, FC or individualistic model. It concerns a mechanism whereby institutions procure and specify services, and it sets up particular, and potentially rigorous, conditions that must be met.

The rigour of the transactions might be helpful if it clarifies needs and ways of meeting them. But it does give anxiety to those acting as providers, for example, schools, as became evident in our consultations. If, for example, a MPP or SPP were to make a contract with a school so as to ensure that pupils received instruction in French, they would need to have a contract that would ensure continuity – why recruit a teacher, prepare a curriculum and buy text books and audio-visual materials for one year only? More difficult, schools have some 'products' for which no account can be made. The calculation involved in X pupils taking and Y passing a one-year course in French, for example, will not extend to many other functions. Pastoral work may involve incalculable time spent on a minority of pupils. In one orderly secondary school it was calculated that one third of senior staff time was spent on 5% of the pupils (Johnson et al, 1980). Would time spent in consultation with parents, or in after school clubs, be allowed for in a contract? Any increase in the intensity of the provider purchaser model would require much reassurance of the sort offered in the Health Service to Trusts, and much closer examination of the level of specification about operations which might well be tested through case law.

Yet another difficulty arises from experience in another field, the NHS. Both purchaser and providers will have to learn and develop new techniques, routines and relationships. There is the problem of the immature provider and purchaser. Moving from intuitive and professional perceptions of needs to be met to the cut and dried specification of them for contractual purposes will involve going deep into issues of objectives and feasibility, as well as of cost.

Modes of democracy

The arguments in favour of government agency models are partly negative evaluations of community agencies. These have been thought by their critics to be wasteful, misdirected and not capable of providing competent democratic inputs into policy making. Attempts to improve political behaviour in education will, however, meet much larger problems of political education among voters and clients, and of achieving effective participation and consultation amongst elected officials. Whilst democratic processes overall are vulnerable to criticism we have to note that there is no structure that is likely to fulfil democratic functions perfectly.

Ministers are legitimated by general elections and they alone are mandated by the political system to take decisions covering the whole national interest. But their capacity to *sustain* legitimacy depends on the extent to which they consult and are in live contact with those who receive the impact of their policies. They are part of a remote democracy which can be made more proximate only if they share power with policy communities who can speak for clients and practitioners and help them test the implementation of their policies. Further legitimacy is afforded to those central authorities which allow competence to a second set of institutions more directly mandated by local electorates. Testing and consultation with intermediary authorities increase the legitimacy of the centre.

Intermediary authorities themselves have similar problems of legitimacy in relation to more local political groupings. LEAs have been shown (e.g. Jennings, 1977) to foreclose on the rights of interest groups to affect local policies. Some have also been destructive of professional leadership (Bush et al, 1989). As shown by the Widdicombe Report (1986), politicisation has become a feature of the working of some local authorities to a point where there is a deficit in consultation about and testing of policies. Some of our interviewees spoke of the remoteness of the county. Others spoke of frustration about LEA governors following a party line and refusing to listen to schools' concerns. Nonetheless, the LEA has legitimacy in being elected by a general electorate, and in being capable of making adjudications of needs for the whole of its area and over the full range of functions; there is, however, undoubtedly a need to improve the processes on which this legitimacy is based.

More local democratic forms are exemplified by the governing body acting perhaps in a LM or GM school or in the even more autonomous format of the individualistic provider. The model of governing body democracy allowed in recent legislation is that of the corporatist state, in which clients are a minority of interests represented in governing bodies; other interests are from categories which are in favour with the central government of the time. But even if the governing bodies were in effect a microcosm of the larger local authority electorate, there is now evidence, including that collected in our study, of the difficulty of governors representing adequately the full client group, of their difficulty in contending with the heavy governance tasks now placed on them, of their difficulty in making a public account, of the unlikelihood that they will take the longer view of needs to be met, and of being capable of placing them in the context of needs to be met by adjacent public services. There is also the difficulty that they both manage a school and are expected to review and criticise it. They may, however, grow into these roles and the take up of places following reconstitution augurs well. LEAs have an important role in facilitating this. But there still remains the problem of linking micro democracy with democratic forms covering wider geographical or stakeholder concerns.

The role of the professional

Cutting across these considerations is the place of the professional in policy making. A government agency model reduces the power of the teacher and administrative professional except within the school itself where the position is negotiable between a head and governing body. It eliminates the strong, if increasingly variable, contribution of the professional at the intermediary level, and possibly at central level, too, where the funding agency is likely to focus more on logistics and resources than on the professional core of the work of the schools. Even within the school, the introduction of the National Curriculum, teacher appraisal, publication of exam results, performance related pay and contract specification all emphasise managerial rather than professional discretion. The head must evince two kinds of professionality: that of the educational leader and that of the chief executive of a provider organisation. General experience is that the managerial tends to drive out or diminish the professional and that propensity is reinforced by the new requirements placed on heads.

All models entail compromise. No model can emphasise all values, needs and functions, partly because of cost, partly because of what is feasible and partly because of conflicts between different values. Systems thus have to reach accommodation between different forms of governance and management. The democratic, managerial and professional perspectives are corners of a triangle of forces. Over time, power distributions change, and it should not be unexpected that a period of strong local and professional rule will be followed by centralisation and de-professionalisation. But any system that does not make an adequate balance between the three is likely to be short of democratic input or expertise or efficiency.

Connections between services

Connection between services has long been an objective of public administration and some of the criticisms made of local government have concerned its failure to secure it. Central government departments and their agencies are unlikely to be able to improve on local authorities in these respects. Only the PE and MPP models are designed to achieve connection.

A further issue is the extent of connection *within* a policy sector. The public agency models assume connection between needs assessment > allocations > planning > implementation > evaluation > monitoring within the system. Under the government models funding, planning and evaluation are placed in different entities; each might attempt all, but in fragmentary fashion. There will be no systematic connection and flow between different aspects of policy making and different levels of knowledge.

The role of the centre

The two sets of models make different assumptions about the power and role of the centre. The community agency model depends on intermediate agencies for the identification of needs and the performance of the requisite functions through the provision and/or the purchase of services and goods. It is likely that there will be a local electoral input into the setting of values and the identification of needs, and that there will be different degrees of the rational planning model with its linking of needs analysis to service specification provision and monitoring.

In the community agency model the centre has key framework functions. It establishes the law, the flow and level of finance, minimum standards in both educational content and provision such as staffing ratios and building standards. It uses these powers and controls to assert national policies on the purposes, structures and size of the educational system. It allows, however, for intermediary bodies to introduce a more local values set and thus to establish their own styles and perceptions of quality and content within very broad national frames. In this formulation, the centre is set in a partnership and leadership role, consulting the main actors in the field and using their experiences and developmental capacity as the starting point for national policy development. The resource at the centre is therefore limited to that necessary for policy framing and monitoring.

In the government agency models, the prime movers in the field are the central authority which either directly or through agents has the determinant say on both the content and the structure of education. It assumes a capacity to read off value preferences for the whole population and to generate sufficient knowledge and information about the impact of policies for it to be able to govern effectively and responsively. The mechanisms by which needs are assessed and the centre informed are not obvious and there is the likelihood of a strong central authority without the connections necessary for competence.

THE EXPRESSIVE AND PSYCHOLOGICAL ASPECTS OF THE MODELS

Systems of governance depend on structure but also on the amount of power and commitment that they can generate. Authority relationships do not themselves determine the way in which systems work. Structures and the authority underpinning them are paralleled by psychological and power relationships. Power – the ability to affect another's behaviour – can be generated not only by the exercise of authority but also by superior knowledge (which might be possessed by a person or entity in a subordinate position), personal charisma, the ability to communicate, obstruct or cooperate, or loyalty.

So drastic a revolution as that implied in the move from community to government agency will mean that many well used networks and established loyalties will be abandoned. This will be reinforced because many who will continue to serve, albeit in different capacities, in the new structures will feel that their earlier work and associations have been subject to derogation and misrepresentation.

Underlying the models are different packages of authority and power. The authority relationships can be simplified as:

- *Managerial authority*. The ability to cause functions to be performed underlies all models. Managerial authority (the authority to instruct and to apply sanctions and rewards) for example underpinned the structure of LEA > head teacher > teacher.

- *Exchange relationship*. This describes a relationship in which accommodations are reached on the exchange of *quids* for *quos*. The implied relationship between and LEA and the DES was primarily of this kind although elements of the managerial were also present. The understanding was that LEAs would perform functions necessary to the achievement of the national goals in return for legitimation and a flow of resources.

- *Market relationships* are a form of exchange relationship.

The *power* relationships invited by the different models can only be estimated. It can be assumed that the relationships entailed in the government agency models, with their emphasis on remote control, will be quite different from those at the other extreme engendered by the more corporate and supporting-controlling ethos of the PE model. The 'market' philosophy will almost certainly advance the psychology of stand-alone pursuit of competitive excellence as against the more cooperative and network making assumptions of the public service models. Purchaser provider relationships may exacerbate the remoteness of government models by emphasising prescription and de-emphasising process. They may, however, add a useful distance and structure to the more local relationships and interests within the community models.

Leadership

Several of our school interviewees spoke of their need for leadership from the larger system. This has meant the performance of such functions as: giving a lead in educational development; authoritative support or action in staff disciplinary cases; convening institutions for exploration of shared problems; interpretation of new laws and circulars or how to cope with financial estimates. In the past, it has involved the advancement of particular educational principles such as those celebrated in progressive primary schools in the 1950s and 1960s and those advanced through TVEI. Even those heads, governors, parents and teachers who looked to reduce intermediary intervention, advice or support in general terms maintained that there was a strong need for collective 'moral leadership'. This might encompass protecting schools, parents and pupils from any levelling down impact from competition on school behaviour towards such issues as admissions, and making manifest a set of local values through which national prescription, such as the National Curriculum, can be interpreted. The role relationship sought appears to be one of influence or power more than structural authority, and represents a move away from the previous relationships held by chief officers. In the past chief officers of LEAs have been both chief executive and professional leader of the LEA service. This entailed the exercise of both authority and power.

Advocacy

Some LEAs are developing an advocacy role. This involves acts on behalf of clients faced with choices offered by providers autonomous of the LEA. It could imply that the LEA makes a needs assessment and evaluates the provision on offer.

The new professionalism

In the new arrangements for educational governance and management, a severely tested component will be that of professionalism.

The definitions of professionalism have included the use of esoteric knowledge, gained by specialised training, and used altruistically for the benefit of clients. The reformed educational system will certainly continue to use specialised knowledge, although the dismantling of professionally run systems of evaluation and advice assumes that it need no longer be esoteric. There will also be altruistic regard for users, sharpened, however, by the need to fulfil contracts.

The new professionalism is likely to involve less a change in the substance of what is provided than in the relationship between provider and purchaser. Providers will no longer deal with dependent clients. Instead clients have purchase over what is provided, always assuming that they know how to use their 'quasi-market' power.

Professionals will thus have to come to terms with the fact that boundaries between provider and client will have become weaker, that professionalism no longer has the same protection from user critique and control. They will have to develop a wider and more energetic approach to discovering clients' wants and converting these to needs. In non elected models, professionals will also need to find substitutes for the functions of both representative democracy (constituency case work) and for the checks and balances and for the expertise in locale provided by elected members.

This will leave the professional with several different tasks to learn to fulfil:

- Educating new controlling and client groups in the fruitful use of their power and authority. The new world will be full of immature customers.
- Ensuring that information for users enhances their exercise of choice.
- Ensuring that the system as a whole benefits from expert evaluation and critique.

The creation of a new professionalism depends on their ability to help clients and the providers who remain to steer their way across new and uncertain boundaries and find new and effective forms for the expression of needs and the underlying values.

These considerations can only be tested as they emerge actively in the educational field. We believe that the criteria suggested in Figure 8.1, together with our frame of values, needs and functions should form the basis of a thorough estimation of the impact of the 1988–1992 reform of British education.

CHAPTER 9

Conclusions and Executive Summary

The latest central initiatives present a decisive break in ways of governing education. Recent legislation affecting LEAs is intended to bring about their virtual replacement.

If local education authorities are thus to disappear, does anything need to take their place? How far can the individual and the autonomous school manage by themselves? What kind of deal might the individual client or the community get if the LEA disappears?

Our study began in the areas of three local authorities where we asked what needs must be met on behalf of individuals, communities and providers, and through which entities they should be met. This led us to a critique of a range of models of governance which we conducted by grading their content in terms of values endorsed, needs met and functions performed. Finally, we raised questions about the modes through which needs are being met, and the nature of the reform processes inaugurated by central government.

We will follow the same sequence in this account of our conclusions.

THE NEEDS TO BE MET

1 Systems driven by needs, rather than existing provision or the offers of providers, are essential for education. At one level or the other, wants and desires have to be transformed into authorised statements of needs. Doing that is contentious and finely balanced between competing legitimate views and beliefs.

2 Individual, community and provider needs must be explored separately because they may conflict. Communities have legitimate needs beyond those of schools and individuals.

3 From our project work, we concluded that there are few absolutely irreducible needs within education; perhaps only ensuring that school places (and the teaching and learning that includes) are provided, and meeting special needs are absolutely essential, and even they would be opposed by de-schoolers. What is irreducible is a matter of political and value choice. But the list of needs becomes quite long when people are asked what they want from education.

The needs of individuals

4 Clients' needs can be grouped as: having a school place (and all that goes with it); providing education for the vulnerable; providing for special educational needs; providing for certain citizens' rights such as the right to appeal against a refusal of place or an expulsion, or the right to complain; and a voice in the control of education. Individuals need help in exercising choices and in identifying needs not previously met. They need access to information and expertise.

Communities' needs

5 Communities have needs based on the value of social cohesion, such as those of democratic representation of their views, of local services which work together and which compete for priority and for a say in major local decisions such as opening and closing schools. There are needs in relation to equity, including the ability to express discontent or problems through established or quasi-judicial channels. There are needs in relation to quality including educational services to be monitored to specified, comparable and locally relevant standards. There are efficiency needs too. Communities need schools to contribute to local economic strength and their agents, for example, Training Enterprise Councils (TECs), need coordinated access. Finally, there are needs in relation to accountability, including a say in the level of funding and for a local public account of local public expenditure.

Providers' needs

6 Some of the providers' needs concern intangibles: for example, the need for schools to work within a collective frame extending well beyond the curriculum and in which connection and leadership can be found. This was endorsed not only by those most committed

to the retention of LEAs but also by some committed to maximum delegation or grant-maintained schools.

7 Many providers, particularly small ones or those facing difficulties, need specialist education services and advice.

8 A somewhat more tangible need felt by heads and governors is that operating the 'market' should not distract from their main tasks. The new arrangements will create immature purchasers and providers, and some with uncertain futures; many providers will look for support and advice on how to work with them. Schools can insure against fire but one head explained how when disaster struck, the LEA had arranged within 24 hours for emergency accommodation, for a planning and maintenance team to get things right.

9 On educational content, many recognise that small schools need advice and support. Large secondary schools, too, some of which have professional staffs larger than many LEA inspectorates, can benefit from good critique and support. Some schools need help to improve from those familiar with their histories.

10 As far as more operational needs of schools are concerned, commissioning school transport might be undertaken by the school, at some cost of administrative time. Pay-roll could be taken over by banks. So too might minor works and maintenance be commissioned.

11 Work requiring continuity and deeper understanding of individual client circumstances, such as educational psychology and school social work, are less likely to benefit from a move to trading relationships. At the very least, an extended period of experimentation and analysis of alternatives would be needed. The needs vary widely between schools and may come in lumps rather than as a regular flow. Both require the capacity to take time to know schools and family environments and perhaps to influence them in ways unlikely to be achieved through time and case limited contracts. Legal work may involve simple conveyancing tasks which can be tendered, but there is a large and constantly changing specialist canon of educational law which takes time to grasp.

12 Providers and communities also have overlapping needs which taken together include: long term planning for future and wider

client groups than those now attending school; leadership and connections between institutions; assurance that schools will not be distracted from their main tasks; external help in remedying as well as identifying faults; room for development and change; and collective arrangements to insure against disaster.

13 On the principle that almost anything can be made to operate, our interviewees were willing to concede that, in the end, the purchasers and providers would learn how to work the new arrangements. But that still left many asking whether the arrangements would work well and why needs must be met in these new ways.

INSTITUTIONS FOR CONTROLLING EDUCATION

14 Control of education is being shifted to centrally appointed bodies and largely autonomous schools. Many believe that education can not be governed by the centre and its appointed quangos in direct control of over 20,000 institutions. Education requires a public service to respond to the geographical, ecological, demographic characteristics and political cultures of diverse areas, as much as to the demands of the centre or small catchment areas.

15 Democratically elected entities may sometimes work inefficiently and be unresponsive but they can be improved by many other techniques advocated in other models, such as market research. Multi-purpose elected bodies have the legitimacy to ensure that local education wants are interpreted as needs and are fully attended to, and that those meeting them give an account of what they have done. The elected base furthermore will provide a stronger possibility that conflicting interests will be resolved through a publicly transparent process.

16 At the same time, new arrangements, such as local management of schools and provider-purchaser relationships, could revivify the governance of education as long as they are conducted within a frame of democratically appointed and multi-purpose bodies. These features of governance are now being canvassed.

MODELS OF GOVERNANCE

17 Several models of educational governance are at present on the political agenda. (Chapters 1 and 4). They can be grouped as

Government Agency Models – those that depend on government appointment – and those that depend on local electoral control – Community Agency Models. We assessed this range of models to see what values they endorse, what needs would be met and what functions would be performed if they were adopted.

18 Community agencies are accountable to local electorates. They include the professional-electoral where power is shared between the teachers, elected members and professional staff of the authority. A multi-purpose purchaser would also be elected to perform functions in a full range of services. It would not provide or manage services but buy them from separate providers. The single purpose public purchaser would be exclusively concerned with education but otherwise be similar to the multi-purpose purchaser. Both purchaser models would assess needs and monitor the services purchased. The individual school board model would also be exclusively concerned with education and would operate rather as GM schools do now (Chapter 4).

19 Government agencies are appointed by central government. They include the unlikely possibility of a wholly centralised system, the funding agency, individualistic and individual school board models. All of these eschew local government and depend upon purchasing arrangements. They endorse school autonomy but are likely to be weak on planning, needs assessment, connection between services and care for those with special needs (Chapter 4).

20 Each of these models is thus likely to yield different treatments of the needs of individuals, communities and providers (Chapter 6).

21 Each model is underpinned by different constellations of values such as individual choice, social cohesion, economic well being and advancement and equality (Chapter 5). For example, individual choice may be advanced by the individualistic models, but not social cohesion or equality which are unlikely to be prominent in the funding agency model either.

22 In comparing the models, the following merits and demerits emerge:

- Present proposals favour the funding agency and the individualistic models of governance. Both eschew planning and democratic input although ultimately a wholly formula driven agency will not work. Judgement will have to be called into play. The individualistic model is weak in tackling special needs.

- Other models are capable of meeting greater ranges of needs, including those of democratic control, needs assessment and connection between services, whilst meeting the challenge of change presented by current legislation.

- An elected, multi-purpose authority using the power to purchase whilst enschewing provision and management could revivify local government. The development of a new market broker role geared to ensuring that gaps are identified and filled would ensure that capacity to meet needs at all levels would be retained.

GENERAL VIEWS EXPRESSED ABOUT THE PATTERNS OF GOVERNANCE

23 Although there were a few dissents, and some questioning of the quality of electoral government, the general belief was that inter-mediary authorities should be democratically accountable to elected rather than to appointed members so that their work will be fully legitimated and so that local educational needs could be fully presented and attended to. There was also, however, a sub-stantial view that elected member roles should be restricted to strategic issues and that an increased input of professional exper-tise was needed; many favoured a mix of elected members and appointed professionals as the board of intermediary authorities.

24 We could find no official statement which argued the case for appointed bodies or assessed their shortfalls. Instead, the case must be inferred on negative evidence about LEAs and their professional employees.

25 It was also seen as right that education should compete for resources with other local services. This was not seen as possible in a system of autonomous schools disconnected from an elected local body.

26 Schools, individuals and communities need systems of governance which will be permeable – capable of being known and influenced by those affected by their actions, including other schools. Present arrangements include autonomous schools under largely non-

elected governing bodies and central quangos appointed by ministers that will not meet this requirement.

27 At the same time, there are merits perceived in many aspects of the new arrangements. They are being adopted, at least in part, and according to the political and professional cultures of different LEAs. There was no dissent from local management of schools (LMS) which has brought greater freedom (and burdens) to schools, and has caused LEAs to rigorously test their values, purposes and functioning. The problems perceived are those of distraction of heads and others from their main educational tasks and the placing of burdens on governors many of whom have not had sufficient training or time to carry them. It is also feared that schools may not retain connection and the leadership hitherto provided by the local authority.

28 Separating provision and purchasing has demonstrable benefits; it enables the needs of both parties to be recognised and met even though they might sometimes conflict. More contentious is the particular version of this arrangement presented in recent legislation. The difficulty arises because the LEA is prevented from acting as purchaser but is held responsible for that which is purchased. Yet schools are required both to provide education and to specify what is provided, in default of any clearly denoted other purchaser. When there are functions which cannot be carried out by individual schools an intermediary body is necessary. In the models where the school is to act as the main purchaser the LEA must be free to offer something worth buying to survive as a provider, but could take on an improved market broker role, even if not allowed to trade.

29 Schools working on funding agency contracts would face difficulties if the contracts are not made with sensitivity about the nature of the services being bought. In specifying quality, volume and cost for contract, there is a danger of breaking up into analytic packages that which is best thought of as integral. A funding agency might attempt to buy by the piece that which should be bought as a whole – integrated academic and pastoral work and relationships with parents are obvious examples. Courses bought by the year rather than for the whole sequence would cause other problems.

30 Yet these quasi-market relationships are perceived by some in LEAs as potentially fruitful. They might emancipate LEAs from the tasks of direct provision and allow them to build up their capacity to assess needs and to monitor the extent to which they are being met whilst assuring themselves that clients' needs are met as to quality, cost and volume. If the purchaser remains part of a multi-purpose, elected and professionally managed entity, many agendas could be met at once and reformed intermediate entities might emerge. Otherwise, the quasi-market arrangements of the funding agency and individualistic working would weaken the holistic and long term thinking which is essential to good education and fail to pay attention to the stakeholder beyond the immediate client groups, or to the needs of future generations of clients.

31 The proposed arrangements could leave the system short of expertise. 'Market' style systems will require a redefinition of professionalism in which professionals must take account of clients' wishes, and empower both clients and providers to make choices. They must move with confidence through new governing arrangements and at the same time make creative contributions to the substance of education – teaching, learning and the recreation of the curriculum. Teachers who used to control their own curriculum have no input to the national curriculum. The drive towards external inspection weakens the opportunities for self-development through self-evaluation.

32 The government agency models are likely to lead to the disconnection of functions that should be connected. Thus, national bodies are concerned separately with resources, inspection, curriculum and examination and the opening and closure of schools. Needs analysis, planning, resourcing and evaluation are being placed with separate entities, if carried out at all. It will then be necessary to make these links in artificial and wasteful ways.

THE CENTRE'S ROLE IN CHANGE AND GOVERNMENT

33 Education needs to be subject to constant challenge, innovation and renewal. Since 1988, however, it has been subject instead to constant disjointed and incomplete experimentation. New practices have not had time to settle down before they have been replaced by yet further attempts to cause change. Whilst the central

authorities have tested other entities rigorously, they have made no provision, nor have parliamentary bodies, for evaluating these drastic reforms.

34 No account has been taken of the enormous loads that the changes will place on the centre. It must govern institutions more directly, take responsibility for the national curriculum and for individual complaints, and inform itself on the effects of its policies and the needs for changing them as they develop. The centralisation of control contrasts with the requirement placed on LEAs to delegate to institutions through LMS.

35 The costs of redundancies, the breaking up of systems, fees for consultants, the costs of a greatly expanded DFE, of creating funding agencies and other centrally appointed bodies, have yet to be accounted for. The costs in human capacity have also to be calculated. Whatever the merits of the reforms, the reduction of LEAs to nullities has been undertaken without deliberation and with a maximum of derogation so as to create a haemorrhage of commitment, expertise and connection.

We conclude by noting that the educational system has been broken up and many new forms of governmental structure created on the basis of evidence that education needs to improve – not on the basis of evidence that the particular aspects of the system to be changed are the cause of the problem or evidence that the changes will improve outcomes. The objectives of the changes often have to be inferred because they are not clearly stated. No provision has been made for the costing and evaluation of the changes.

In Chapter 6 we have suggested that the educational needs of three distinct groups should be the basis for education governance.

In Chapter 8 we have suggested some of the additional criteria by which the changes can be evaluated. The lavish expenditure of public money at a time of economic duress ought to draw the attention of the House of Commons Public Accounts Committee where enquiry should be backed by an exigent study by the National Audit Office. That no such proposal has been made underlines the weakness of the political responses to the measures promoted by the government.

The remaining, and equally important, criteria for evaluation concern such wide ranging issues as the quality of education that will ensue from the destruction of LEAs, the degrees of autonomy that will in fact be enjoyed by the school, the quality of professionalism in the schools, and the quality of client participation and democratic control.

We hope that these matters will not be allowed to pass by without the proper level of public notice and critique.

References

Arnstein, S. (1969) 'A Ladder of Citizen Participation', *Journal of the American Insitute of Planners*, Vol 35.

Audit Commission, (1989) 'Losing an Empire and Finding a Role, the LEA of the Future'. London:HMSO.

Bush, T. Kogan, M. and Lenney, T. (1989) *Directors of Education – Facing Reform.* London: Jessica Kingsley.

DFE White Paper (1992) *Choice and Diversity: A New Framework for Schools*, Cm 2021. London: HMSO.

Hampton, W, (1987) *Local Government and Urban Politics.* Harlow: Longman.

Herbert Report, (1960) *Report of Royal Commission on Local Government in Greater London.* Cmnd. 1164. London: HMSO.

Jennings, RE. (1977) *Educational Politics: Policy Making in Local Education Authorities.* Batsford.

Johnson, D. Ransom, E. Packwood, T. Bowden, K. and Kogan, M. (1980) *Secondary Schools and the Welfare Network.* Unwin Education Books.

Mill, J.S. (1912) *Considerations on Representative Government.* Oxford: Oxford University Press, (quoted by Sharpe, see below).

Packwood, T. and Whitaker, T. (1988) *Needs Assessment in Post 16 Education.* Brighton: Falmer.

Plowden Report, (1967) Central Advisory Council of Education (England), *Children and their Primary Schools.* London: HMSO.

Ranson, S. (1992) *The Role of Local Government in Education: Assuring Quality and Accountability.* Harlow: Longman.

Lord Redcliffe-Maud and Bruce Wood, (1974) *Local Government Reformed.* Oxford: Oxford University Press.

Redcliffe-Maud Report, (1969) *Royal Commission on Local Government in England*, Cmnd 4040. London: HMSO.

Rein, M. (1983) *From Policy to Practice.* London: Macmillan.

Sharpe, L.J. (1970) 'Theories and Values of Local Government', *Political Studies*, Vol.XVIII, Oxford: Clarendon Press.

Stewart, J. (1991) *Local Democracy – Representation and Elections.* Belgrave Paper no 1, Local Government Management Board.

Widdicombe Report, (1986) *The Conduct of Local Authority Business. Report of the Committee of Inquiry into Local Government Business*, Cmnd 9797. London: HMSO.

Questionnaire used in Field Studies

1   What education functions need to be fulfilled by a public agency beyond the level of the provider?

Why should they be done by the LEA –	Which alternative agencies might do it:
possible justifications:	
Concentration of expertise	National authority
Economy of scale	Providers taking collective action
Democratic control/social justice	Other public agencies
Overview	Other private agencies
Other	Other means

A1 What services need to be provided to the individual pupil, student and parent, beyond the level of the individual institution?

Function	Justification	Other agencies
Careers services		
Psychological and counselling services		
Access to schools		
Information about schools and other levels of education		
Direct payments for uniforms, meals		
Payment of Higher Education mandatory and discretionary awards		
Statementing		
School transport		
Enforcement of school attendance		
Access to appeals procedures		
Quality assurance about services		
Political representation and expression		
Ensuring efficient self-management of the Local Authority		

A2 On the assumption that there are a range on educational and related community needs which range beyond the individual school area, what services need to be provided to the community / locale beyond the level of the individual institution?

Function	Justification	Alternative agency
Equality: Distribution of educational resources throughout the system		
Analysis of needs over and beyond those provided by schools individually		
Ensuring comprehensiveness and consistency between provisions between schools and other providers		
Allocation of different functions to different providers in a coherent way		
Providing connecting links between pre-school, primary and secondary schools, FE and other providers		
Attending to a prosperity. Ensuring there is capital and plant and a secure place in which education provision will continue to be provided for future generations		
Expert services and advice at the community level		
Appeal provision (e.g. on closure of schools)		
Social reporting and auditing and evaluation		
Evaluating provision made by non-public providers		
Local political expressive function		

A3 Services to providers

Function	Justification	Alternative Agency
Assessment of needs and information about them so that they can provide services and market them		
External evaluation of their quality		
Provision of resources, both capital and recurrent		
Linkages with other services		
Providing advice and guidance on curriculum and education		
Providing advice and guidance on maintaining services		
Providing advice and guidance on personnel control and other matters		
Financial information		
Inset		
Providing planning frames and school development planning		
Building and estates management advice		
Advice on legal matters		
Advice on appointments		
Convening cooperation between providers		
Operating the payroll		
Other direct services such as supplies, possibly through purchasing consortia or other arrangements		
Management services; computing and IT		
Specialist curriculum provision		

A4 What services need to be provided to central government?

Function	Justification	Alternative Agency
Providing data		
Administration of schemes		
Monitoring of implementation of national legislation on appraisal, curriculum, etc.		
Administration of higher education statutory awards		

Index